ESSEX
UNDER ARMS

the early years to 1900

Ken Smith

Ian Henry Publications

© K G Smith, 1998
ISBN 0 86025 490 9

Published by
Ian Henry Publications, Ltd.
20 Park Drive, Romford, Essex RM1 4LH
and
printed by
Interprint, Ltd.
Industrial Estate, Marsa HMR 15, Malta

Chapter 1
Early days - Iron Age and Pre-Roman Essex

Henry V, through the words given him by Shakespeare, inspired the English soldiers before Harfleur in 1415, with this stirring exhortation, 'Cry 'God for Harry, England and Saint George!''

In Essex, nearly four hundred and twenty five years earlier, Ælfwine, a soldier 'young in winters', tried to rally his fellow thegns (thanes) - Old English word for 'someone who was part of the king's, or a lord's, household or a member of his fighting force' - after the death of their leader, Byrhtnoth, at the Battle of Maldon. He said, with words not so well remembered, 'Think of all the times we boasted at the mead-bench, heros in the hall predicting our own bravery in battle. Now we shall see who meant what he said.' These challenging words appear to have had the desired effect on his colleagues even if they might not have the same resonance on us today.

Here are two different ways of encouraging the common soldier in the cause for which he is fighting and encouraging him to be brave in the face of the enemy. However, Ælfwine's poetic words to his colleagues were likely to be more effective for the simple reason that these warriors were fighting to protect their own homes and families, in Essex. The attack was coming from the Danes who had been terrorising the coast from Sandwich to Ipswich, before returning south to Maldon.

The Battle of Maldon was one of many bloody battles that took place at sites around Essex - it was not the first, and it certainly was not the last. This particular battle was made famous by being recorded in the Anglo-Saxon Chronicle and in the epic poem of the same name.

Due to its geographical position facing east opposite the large land mass of Europe, and with its flat coast line, Essex has always been one of the counties forming the first line of defence for attack from that quarter. It is also in the forefront of any immigration from people travelling over from the continent to settle. Bounded to the north by the Stour, the south by the Thames, and to the east by the North Sea, Essex as a result has featured prominently in wars and battles over the centuries. The sandbanks off-shore that restrict movement of commercial shipping, militarily protects the coastline by only allowing boats to approach through the river estuaries, and these rapidly slim down into streams-again restricting movement of any attacker moving further inland.

Even a 1000 years before this attack by the Danes, Essex people were having to defend their land, homes and lives by the sword. The trend for fighting, violence, and a military presence, in order to protect possessions or a way of life, has continued to the present day.

Was there life in Essex during the Palæolithic, or Old Stone Age (around 8000 BC)? If so, when did man come to the area?

Tools of this period, in the form of hand axes, together with fossilized bones, have been found at various sites in the county, such as a gravel pit at Canewdon, and farms at Barling and Rochford. Whether they resulted from man and animals living in the locality, or whether they were the spoils of rivers carried downstream by the current and deposited, is not known.

One of the earliest sites to have a defensive function is considered to be Orsett Causewayed Enclosure. It was discovered during 1973 from crop-marks, described as 'three irregular concentric circuits of interrupted ditches'. The inner ditch measured between 80 m to 90 m across, with a gap of 30 m to 40 m to the next, while the outer circuit lay a further 10 m away.

Most of the evidence following on from this period, particularly in the south of the county, appears to indicate temporary residence rather than permanent occupation. which occurred around 650 BC. This lack of evidence could mean that no information has yet been found to show otherwise. Again experts say that not too much is known about Neolithic and Bronze Age settlements because they were not defended by a surrounding bank and ditch. However, it is possible they have not been recognised and excavated.

In general the Bronze Age saw a major change in the way men fought with the introduction of the sword, a double-edged heavy weapon used for slashing, which displaced the older rapier - a small sword for thrusting. And the bronze shield made an appearance. During the Iron Age period, when iron weapons - and implements - were being introduced, a community depending on the metal for its survival emerged at Sheepen.

Evidence exists to indicate that people were crossing the Channel bringing about an apparent increase in trade with the continent. Many of these travellers were immigrants who came from northern France and used natural features, such as the Thames, Crouch, Blackwater and Colne for landing in the area. However, as the estuaries narrow quickly and soon dwindle into streams they did not afford the travellers rapid movement into the interior of the county.

New settlers brought their customs and skills with them, which were gradually absorbed by the indigenous population. Essex at this period was still mainly covered by the primæval forest. These woods extended from the coast to the Chiltern Hills - Hockley and Rayleigh Woods, together with Epping Forest are remnants. The newcomers were soon competing with the existing inhabitants for the fertile grazing lands concentrated along the river valleys. Other desirable plots were areas of forest cleared of trees and undergrowth. Evidence shows that fighting was a popular method of securing these highly prized areas of land.

As a result of this increasing pressure on easily cultivated land, the native population began to introduce some form of security to protect what they held. They started to build defended forts, which, if they were to be ideally situated, would be on a hill top. Due to the fact that there are not too many hills and the area is mainly low-lying land, not too many hill forts are to be found in Essex or Suffolk.

That these times must have been fairly violent in the Essex region, and that the inhabitants wanted to hold on to the possessions they already had, is shown by the fact that single farmsteads and isolated villages were protected by ditch and palisade defences. Examples have been found at Mucking and Heybridge, while larger settlements secured by ditches and banks have been found at Prittlewell and Stambridge. It is possible, however, that these were only temporary strongpoints built as shelters for villagers and stock between 50 BC and AD 43.

During this period Essex was inhabited by the powerful tribe of the Trinovantes, whose territory covered an area at least from modern Colchester to the mouth of the Thames. The western boundary is thought to be in Hertfordshire, but the northern boundary is more difficult to determine. It is highly unlikely that the boundaries between neighbouring tribes were precisely defined, and it is probable that skirmishes helped one side or the other to gain territorial advantage. The situation did not stabilise until the Romans came and settled.

The Trinovantes' traditional enemy were the neighbouring Catuvellauni who lived to the west with their capital thought to be at Wheathampstead, near St Albans, Hertfordshire. Against this back-ground many communities were building and moving into strongly fortified hill forts as a means of protection. Today the remains of these strongpoints are a characteristic feature of the period.

A number lie in the south and west of the county in the area of Epping Forest, around Loughton Camp and Ambresbury Banks and further north at Wallbury. However, no large scale excavations have been carried out at these sites to determine the facts.

Loughton Camp occupies an area of 4.6 ha. It stands on a promontory with the land falling sharply away on the south and south west. A single bank and ditch protected the site.

Small scale excavations at Ambresbury Banks, probably the highest point in the forest, have indicated that the fort had first been built in the fifth century BC, although there are indications that the site was occupied before then, but not defended. It is said that Ambresbury Banks occupied an area of 4.5 ha and was protected by a rampart and ditch with a small counterscarp - a steep slope-bank. The entrance on the west side was carefully revetted, or faced, with dry stone walling. Considering the tools available, construction must have taken a substantial time as the ditch was said to be 3 m deep, 6.5 m wide and the slope from the bottom of the ditch to the top of the bank was 6 m.

Also dating from this period is the 75 m diameter bi-vallate (double wall) hillfort overlooking the Thames at Mucking.

Wallbury was a larger fort overlooking the river Stort, covering some 12.5 ha. Its defences were in part of a natural barrier of marshy land reinforced on the river side with a single rampart and in the remaining sectors with a double rampart and ditch. The east and west entrances are rather unusual. They are said to indicate that the camp was not only suitable for defence, but could be used to shelter warriors before they emerged in great numbers to attack the opposing forces.

To the east and slightly south of Chelmsford is the hillfort of Danbury. It stands on a prominent hill commanding a magnificent view across central and south-east Essex. Danbury's part in Essex history at this period remains a mystery. The site and the still prominent single bank and ditch defending the fort have not been excavated. Unfortunately, construction of roads, the church and rectory, and modern cultivation have destroyed many traces of the defences.

A single bank and ditch afforded safety at Uphall Camp at Ilford. However, it is possible that this work - together with similar forts at Prittlewell and South Weald - was post-Roman. Also said to be post-Roman are the Saffron Walden war ditches.

Three other defended areas where dates for construction are uncertain are Asheldham, Downham (Grange), and Ring Hill (Littlebury). Asheldham is in the Dengie Hundred and is thought to have been constructed during the Iron Age. The site, occupying 6.5 ha, managed to remain in existence during the Roman occupation to be resurrected by the Saxons as a defensive position. Pottery and weapons, namely a knife and a Danish type throwing axe dating from about the ninth century were unearthed in the ditch. The hillfort was of the univallate, or single wall type.

Downham Grange, near Billericay, again thought to be of Iron Age construction, protected the area from assault from the south-west, north-east and east. This site also survived Roman occupation and was utilised by the Saxons; unfortunately no remains can be seen today.

South of Littlebury church in the north west of the county lie the remains of Ring Hill Camp, which occupied about 6.6 h. The defences are said to have consisted of a rampart and a ditch about 15 m wide and 15 m deep. The entrances have not been located.

A fort at Witham is said to date from Saxon times. Protected by a ditch and a substantial rampart, the fort was possibly built in the tenth century as a defence against the Danes by Edward the Elder.

Valuable historical evidence is to be found with the discovery of coins. The distribution of coins provide details of who was living where and at what time. Additionally, they also give an indication of the political situation at the time-whether the tribes were at war, living in peace, or if one tribe had occupied the other's territory. (Although it does not apply during this period, seals on documents also render valuable evidence.)

Settlers began arriving around this period and were known as the Belgae. Imported gold coins, brought by traders or settlers from an area in France between the Seine and the Somme, dating from about 125 BC (called Gallo-Belgic A) indicate the first contact with these people. Although the majority are found in Kent, a number have been found scattered in north Essex. Around 100 BC a fresh batch of gold coins (Gallo-Belgic C) appeared on the scene carried in by additional newcomers who made their homes in Kent. This latest group appear to have had difficulty in penetrating into Essex, possibly because the natives prevented this happening. As a result coins from this period are scarce in the county.

Additionally the Belgic used a different form of protection for sites. Although they were familiar with hill-forts they generally lived in low-lying areas, mainly because most of the hilltop sites were denied to them. To defend these large areas containing their farms and lands, known as oppida, they built immense linear dykes.

Forty five years later, in 55 BC, Caesar landed in England with a force of about 10,000 men, but the expedition ended in failure. The Romans were the first to invade Britain and write about the event. Two major developments followed that invasion. First, whatever happened in Britain from this period would start to be recorded in writing. Major events would be described and comments made. No longer would there be a complete silence on what was taking place. Secondly, a calendar enters the human story and dates start to become a means of charting what is happening at various times in the known world.

The Romans were well aware of Britain before they invaded the country, and they also knew that trade existed between the island and the continental mainland. The Roman leaders knew the island people were not united and that 'warring factions' existed among the various tribes. In fact, Tacitus described the people living in Britain as 'barbarians'.

In his invasion reports *De Bello Gallico*, Caesar mentions the Trinovantes, a tribe part of whose territory included Essex. In 54 BC Caesar returned with a much stronger force of 25,000 foot soldiers consisting of detachments from five legions, together with 2,000 cavalry and contingents of slingers and archers. He is thought to have entered the area that later became Essex, by crossing the Thames at low water somewhere in the Westminster area near London. During this second invasion his main opponents were the Catuvellauni, and Caesar's main objective was to attack their capital, Wheathampstead. The Catuvellauni lived in what is now Hertfordshire and their arch enemy, the Trinovantes, were now Caesar's allies.

How was it that the Trinovantes came to be on the side of the Romans if they were the major force in the area? It appears that the Catuvelauni shortly before Caesar's invasion had attacked the Trinovantes and murdered the king. As a result, Mandubracius, the king's youngest son and heir, fled to Rome to seek protection and ask for help in regaining his lands and people. Caesar returned and successfully stormed the Catuvellauni capital. He accepted their surrender and their promise to pay a yearly tribute, but it appears not a single denarius was ever paid.

Once again when Caesar left Britain the Trinovantes and the Catuvellauni returned to their old ways and continued hostilities. First one side was victorious and then the other. Around 17 BC, Addedomarus, ruler of the Trinovantes, seems to have been evicted from Colchester by Tasciovanus, king of the Catuvellauni. The reason the experts came to this conclusion is that Tasciovanus commenced to use the mint, already located at Colchester, to produce coins bearing his name and the letters CAMV an abbreviation of Camulodunum (Colchester). The name is derived from dunum or fortress of Camulos, a Celtic war god. However, Tasciovanus's occupation stay was short lived and Addedomarus returned once again.

Tasciovanus, in turn, was replaced by Dubnovellaunus, formerly ruler of Kent. Due to lack of evidence it is unknown whether he succeeded to the position legally, or won the title in battle. What is known, however, from the records of the Emperor Augustus, is that by AD 7 he had fled to Rome. He arrived in Italy as an exile and suppliant, possibly as a result of the son of Tasciovanus, Cunobelin, assembling an army and driving him out.

Around AD 7 Tasciovanus died and was succeeded by Cunobelin. He is probably the best known of any British character so far encountered, ruling most of south east England by the end of his reign. The Romans called him 'King of the Britons', and Shakespeare called him Cymbeline. Experts now generally accept that the Trinovantes were overrun by the Catuvellauni tribe, and that Cunobelin moved his capital from Verulamium (St Albans) to Camulodunum, where he very quickly established himself. Cunobelin quickly ordered coins to be minted. Examples bearing his name on the obverse and the mint mark for Colchester on the reverse are still plentiful throughout Essex. Excavation at Sheepen in recent years unearthed the remains of the clay moulds in which the coins were cast.

Coins bearing the Cunobelin name and dated from AD 25 have been discovered in Kent. From this evidence it is assumed that he was now ruling Kent from his base at Colchester.

Colchester occupied 32.5 km² and was extremely well defended. Although there is evidence of earlier occupation, as described above, the defences and structures that have been uncovered are recognisable as dating from the first century AD.

The defences were massive linear dykes which the experts say were 'unparalleled in strength elsewhere in Britain'. Professor Hawkes who made a special study of the subject, says the Heath Farm Dyke curvilinear rampart defences overlooking the Roman river are the earliest in the scheme. They are unusual in that they did not set the trend for the later defences, which were straight, instead following the north, west and south sides of a small headland, or promontory.

Sheepen Hill, above the Colne valley marshes, appears to be the main area where people lived in Cunobelin's reign. He defended the area by erecting three widely spaced ramparts, of which only the filled in ditch of the Sheepen Dyke, the innermost one, remains. The V-shaped ditch was said to be 12 m wide at the top and 3 m deep. A similar ditch formed the Lexden Dyke, stretching northwards for around 2.5 km. It is about 1 km west of the Hill and, in its heyday, could have extended further in both easterly and southerly directions.

About 1 km further west was a third ditch, the Shrub End Dyke. Evidence of a fourth ditch, called the Barn Hall Dyke, has been unearthed to the east and south of the latter two ditches. Originally all the ditches would have had sturdy ramparts. We are told that traces exist of wooden gateways through the Lexden and Sheepen Dykes and that along the top of the ramparts were timber palisades.

Modifications were continually made to the defences over the course of time. Eventually the complex was completed and surrounded by another tremendous construction extending for 5 km. This is known as Grimes Dyke, whose ramparts today still stand around 2 m high.

Rosalind Dunnett in *The Trinovantes*, as well as providing a good description of the defences around Sheepen, mentions the Belgic cemetery at Lexden, unearthed when the Victorian suburbs were being built. During excavation the hacked-up remains of iron chainmail which had originally been riveted to a backing, possibly leather, was discovered. Unfortunately, like so many of the other finds in the grave it had been broken into small fragments. Whether this was part of the burial ceremony or the work of later grave robbers is not known.

However, it would appear that during the reign of Cunobelin, Essex and all his territory enjoyed nearly forty years of independence. That situation was to change when he died in AD 40 and the kingdom was shared between his two sons, Togodumnus and Caratacus. Within three years Claudius launched an invasion of Britain, mainly as a result of an appeal to him from Verica, king of the Atrebates of Sussex, whose kingdom had been overrun in AD 42 by Caratacus and Togodumnus. The outcome was that Essex, and in particular Colchester, was to witness some violent and bloodthirsty fighting.

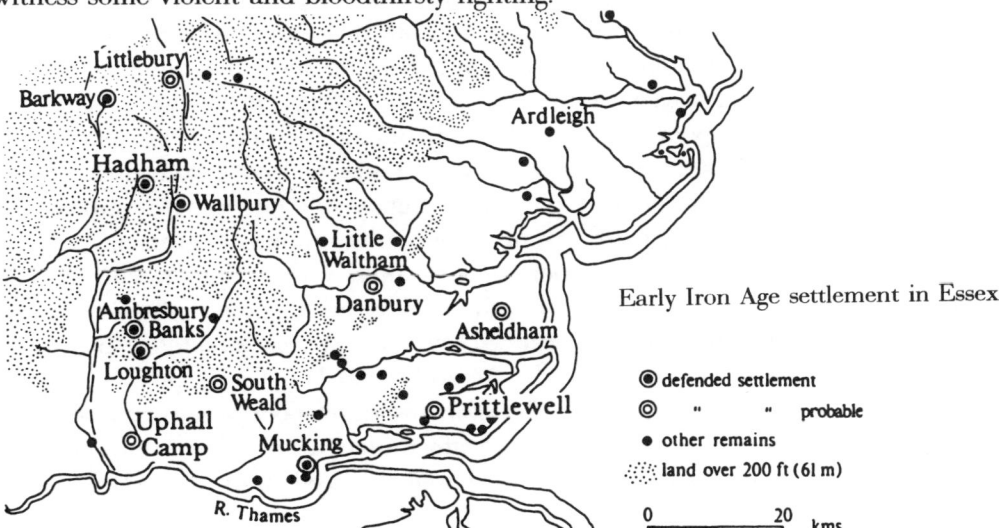

Early Iron Age settlement in Essex

◉ defended settlement
◎ "   " probable
● other remains
land over 200 ft (61 m)

0 — 20 kms

Chapter 2
The Romans return

A hundred years after Caesar had left the Romans returned in strength. In AD 41, due mainly to the army's support and loyalty, Claudius became Emperor after the murder of his nephew, Caligula. His position was insecure and, being purely a politician, he lacked glory from any military successes. To survive he needed a triumph and Britain seemed an obvious, and the easiest, place to win one.

An invasion force of four legions, led by Aulus Plautius, was assembled. They were the II Augusta, who had been stationed on the Rhine at Strasbourg, the XX Valeria Victrix from the Lower Rhine, from the Middle Rhine came the XIV Gemina, and from Panonia came the IX Hispana. The legions were supported by a large number of auxiliary troops comprising cavalry, archers, slingers and many others from provinces in the Roman Empire, such as Thrace and Gaul.

A large number of the veteran campaigners in the attacking force believed that Britain was on the edge of the known world. As a result they were not keen to embark on this expedition, even though there was glory to be had in simply crossing the 'ocean'. The total number of men involved in the invasion was some 50,000. Among the commanders was a future Emperor, Vespasian, who led the II Augusta.

The basis of the Roman Army was the legion and the total number allowed were strictly controlled and never allowed to exceed 35. Each legion, defined by a number, consisted of 5,000 heavy infantrymen. These troops were well disciplined and trained to overcome the enemy in hand-to-hand fighting with set-piece battles. For relaying messages, scouting and cavalry duties there were about 120 lightly armed horsemen. In overall charge was a Senator, supported by six officers, or military tribunes, who were young men of importance beginning the first stage of their political careers by serving in the army. Beneath them were 60 centurions.

Besides being a self-contained fighting unit a legion also incorporated a large number of craftsmen and specialists in fields able to assist in achieving a successful outcome of the military operation. As well as including the ubiquitous clerks there were armourers, carpenters, glaziers, medical attendants, hydraulic specialists, stone-masons, surveyors, and possibly river pilots and shipwrights among its numbers. All these experts would lift the total strength of the legion to around 6000 men.

The legionary, or individual soldier, at this time was a Roman citizen. His uniform consisted of a helmet equipped with cheek-pieces to protect the face, while bronze or iron segmented plates, known as the *loricasegmentata*, provided protection for the upper part of his body. As additional body protection he carried a semi-cylindrical shaped long shield. The Romans developed various manoeuvres, using the shield, to provide a group defence against attack from in front and above.

He was armed with two main weapons, a well-balanced throwing javelin, called a *pillim*, equipped with a long iron point, which would be used first while the enemy was still at a distance from him. The second item was a short sword, called a *gladius*, which was used in hand-to-hand fighting for cutting and thrusting.

A leather jerkin, which reached to his knees, was worn beneath his armour, while on his feet he wore leather boots, called caligae. These gave rise to their nickname of 'foot-sloggers', derived from the Latin *caligatae*, which translated means those who wore the caligae.

At this period to overcome the restrictions in the number of legions allowed, auxiliary soldiers were recruited from one particular area such as the Middle East, Crete or the Balearic islands. These men from the frontier regions were, in general, non-Roman citizens and their special skills were as archers, slingers, and cavalry, while there was an infantry group, whose mission was to act as scouts, guard prisoners, plunder and burn. Auxiliaries served for 25 years. This was the basis of the army that was to protect Britain for the next 400 years.

On reaching Britain the Romans landed at several points, possibly to conceal the fact that the main attack was centred on Rutupiae (Richborough). Although the landings took place in Kent, indications are that Camulodunum, across the Thames to the north, was the major objective of the Roman invasion.

Opposing this invasion force were the British led by Caratacus and Togodumnus, the sons of Cunobelin. On Cunobelin's death his kingdom had been split in two with Caratacus reigning over the western area of Surrey, Hampshire and Middle Thames, while Togodumnus ruled the Essex and Hertfordshire area. This division is thought by the experts to have a bearing on the outcome after the first major battle.

This initial conflict on the Medway, possibly near Rochester, lasted two days, with victory going to the Romans. The Britons then retreated to the Thames. It was around this area that Togodumnus was killed in a skirmish and in the confusion as to who was to replace him, the Romans were able to secure a bridgehead on the northern shore of the Thames.

Here the Romans paused to await the arrival of Claudius, who arrived six weeks later with reinforcements - his Praetorian guard and, it is reported, elephants. The final march towards Camulodunum could now begin, through Chelmsford and Kelvedon, where Claudian military fortifications have been unearthed.

This pause by the Romans enabled Caratacus to unify his position as leader of the British forces. By the time Claudius was ready to lead his men on the march to Colchester, Caratacus had been able to reassemble his forces and a second battle took place. The Britons were again defeated. Caratacus escaped to Wales, leaving a victorious Claudius free to enter Camulodunum, and to receive the submission of the town and a number of neighbouring tribes - said by some experts to amount to eleven. After only sixteen days Claudius departed for Rome leaving orders for the governor to conquer the rest of Britain.

As the campaigning season was nearly over the main concern for Plautius was to decide where to locate the bulk of the army during the winter. Although a number of troops would be garrisoned in forts along the line of advance through Kent and Essex and other occupied areas, the vast majority would probably be still in the Colchester area. It is highly likely that a semi-permanent camp was built here that first winter, which later became established as a fortress. For some years after the victory the site became the headquarters of the Roman administration.

Immediately after the celebrations were over the Romans set about strengthening the defences of the area. It would appear that the Triple Dyke, 3 km west of Colchester, was constructed as a temporary structure around this time. If this was the case then the entire site was protected by natural features, such as the marshland and the river Colne to the north, the Triple Dyke to the east, to the south was Peartree Dyke and to the west was the vast Grimes Dyke.

It has been suggested that the area enclosed by these features is very reminiscent of the site at Richborough, which the Romans used for a limited period as a bridgehead during the invasion, and could, therefore, have been ideal to temporarily house the garrison for the winter months following the victory.

Camulodunum became the capital of the Roman province for a short period. It offered many advantages to the conquerors. Reasons why the early settlers selected the site for a major centre in the first place still applied for the Romans. It could be readily defended, it was on a river close to the sea, it provided a ready link to other areas to the south, to the continent and back to Rome. Land communications to the rest of the country occupied by the Romans were good, so troops could be rapidly moved around to where they were needed.

However, the location of any permanent fort within the area is still the subject of much debate. Finds at Fingringhoe of imitation Claudian coins and quantities of military equipment possibly indicate that some sort of supply depôt, or base, was situated there, and that there was a major camp somewhere in the locality.

Another site to acquire town status was Great Chesterford. Like Colchester it was initially defended with earthworks; sometime later walls were built. Sadly, it did not get the prominence that Colchester achieved.

Once it emerged that the south-east had been subdued the Romans began to consolidate the area. It was important to garrison the north bank of the Thames estuary, which being a major supply route from the continent, it was essential to keep open. To achieve this it was necessary to build roads, and as far as possible these were surveyed and constructed by the army. Most of the unskilled labouring and semi-skilled work would probably be done by the ordinary legionary, while there were others who were trained in specialised skills, such as road building and erecting fortifications, as well as fighting. The primary task of the legionary was soldiering and he was a tradesman second.

To be effective, policing the area would depend on a network of forts and camps within a reasonable distance, possibly a day's march from Colchester. Tracks radiating from the administrative capital would lead to these defensive positions, to carry troops and supplies. This probably accounts for the marching camp noticed by aerial observation in growing crops at Hadleigh in early 1949. Its size of approximately 250 ft^2 makes it suitable for a cohort of 500 men. It would have been of strategic importance overlooking the Thames estuary. As the site has not been excavated it is impossible to say when it was built.

Some experts think that on major roads there were posts or relay stations situated every eight to 15 miles. Here at the end of a day's march there was scope for the legionaries to have hot baths, while the post was capable of handling changes of horse at any time of the day or night. Others suggest they would be located every 25 miles.

So far only a few of these forts have been identified positively. Whatever figure is used there remain a large number of forts to be discovered in Essex. Kelvedon is one where excavation has taken place. During the work military ditches were traced and various military finds and pottery from the Claudian period were unearthed. The site lies between the river Blackwater and the modern village.

Chelmsford, or Caesaromagnus, implying imperial connections with Caesar, is another area where evidence of military occupation has been discovered. This site is located close to where the London-Colchester road crosses the river Can. About 200 m further south was discovered a Claudian military ditch, said to be associated with a fort established on slightly higher ground in the area. Little is known of its history or character, especially as the adjacent low lying area is prone to flooding - unless at this period the river was navigable up to that point.

Other forts in the south of the county include Orsett, with an area about 0.8 ha, defended by a rampart and a double ditch. Wickford, opened by excavators in 1971, dates from the Claudian era. It is thought to be a marching camp, a temporary fort, possibly built during the initial invasion.

Dating from the same period is a small earthwork at Mucking. Due to military finds during excavations and its closeness to the Thames, it is thought the site may have military connections. Aerial photographs have revealed rectangular defended enclosures indicating additional locations where Roman camps could have existed; these include East and West Tilbury. Another possibility, according to some experts, is Maldon. To the west of Colchester, on the road to St Albans, troops must have been garrisoned.

Although considerable quantities of Roman remains have been discovered, it has not been possible to establish a direct link between them and any military forts. A similar situation exists at Dunmow where yet again it has proved impossible to confirm a connection between Roman occupation and a fort.

Again, to the north of Colchester on the boundary between the two tribes, the Trinovantes and the Suffolk/Norfolk based Iceni, one would expect forts to be in evidence. Signs of military occupancy have been found at Great Chesterford with the unearthing of a large fort with protection for half a legion. The site lies to the north of the later Roman town and occupies an area of 14 to 15 ha. However, the finds that were uncovered during the excavation indicate that the stronghold was built after the Boudiccan revolution.

It is possible that in the post-conquest period, the Trinovantian survivors that remained in the area, and did not escape to the west with Caratacus, were cowed into submission.

Evidence from excavations shows that many of the able-bodied men were rounded up under military supervision and kept at Colchester in 'works depôts'. Excavation has also shown that a huge influx in population occurred in the Sheepen Hill area in the immediate after-math of the conquest. This was particularly so in the area housing rows of small workshops capable of producing metal work. Here additional local labour could have been used, under surveillance, to make the various metal items of military equipment found during excavation of the rubbish pits, such as pieces of helmet, cuirass hooks, bronze buckles and numerous imitation bronze coins used by the soldiers.

By the time Aulus Plautius left Britain for Rome in AD 47 the entire area to the south of a line drawn from the Wash to the Severn had been crushed. Camulodunum's importance as a military base had diminished as troops were withdrawn to support the battlefronts in the west. Tacitus mentions that the XXth legion was sent from Colchester to Gloucester. However, as an extra precaution the tribes living in the eastern lowland region were disarmed.

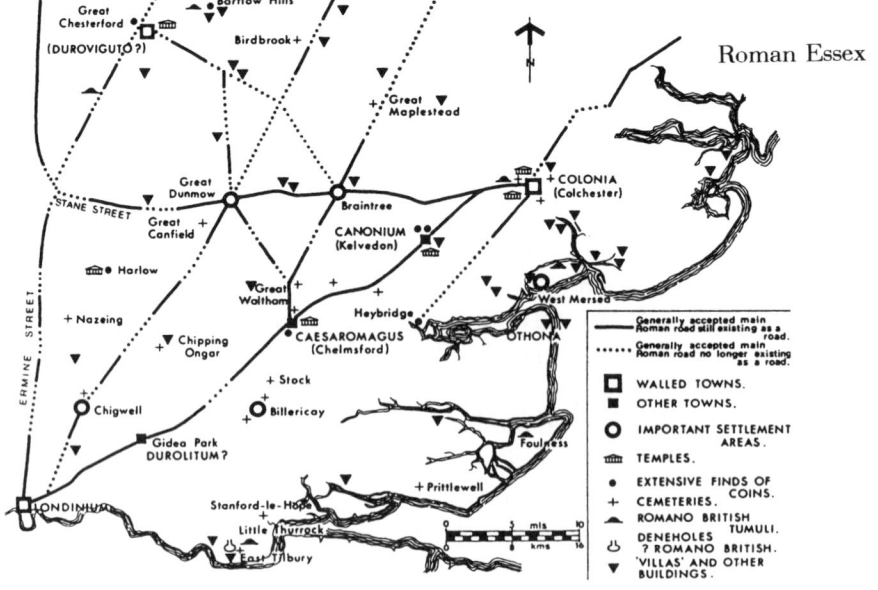

Chapter 3
Boudicca meets the Romans

Aulus Plautius was succeeded by Ostorius Scapula, who was Governor of Britain from AD 47 to 51-2. He made changes which were to have far reaching effects on the Roman occupied territories. An important point to remember here is that the effect of events on the ordinary people is often more forbidding, and more severe than was intended by the originator, and those in power who initiated the policies.

Scapula's policy in AD 47 was to consider the area to the south of a line drawn from the Trent to the Severn as pacified. For this to be effective the Romans needed to disarm all of the tribes in the area. The result on the local population was that it could only carry weapons for protection on long journeys, or for hunting. Scapula also attempted to establish Roman authority over the Iceni, whose territory lay to the east of the Trent. This tribe up until this period had been allowed to govern itself, although dependent on Roman power for defence. It was the Norfolk Iceni, who was one of the leading tribes to resist disarmament, and who gave battle. Some years later it was to do so again under Boudicca.

In AD 49, the Roman forces advancing westward into Wales in an endeavour to conquer the rest of Britain, met strong resistance and needed reinforcements. The Romans once again had met Caratacus, for it was to Wales that Caratacus had fled after his defeat in Essex, and where he found new allies who would help him continue his opposition.

He was to remain a thorn in the Roman's side for a further eight years. Eventually, Caratacus was captured and sent to Rome, where they generously granted him a pardon.

Tacitus gives an indication that the XXth legion was sent from Colchester as reinforcement, and that it arrived in the Gloucester area at the end of the year.

Although the garrison around Colchester must have been greatly depleted as a result of this exodus, the Romans would have ensured there were sufficient troops available to keep the peace. Even the local forts scattered around the canton would have maintained a token force, albeit on a reduced scale.

At about this same time, AD 49/50, at Camulodunum a colonia, or chartered town, was being founded, which the Romans felt would strengthen their hold over the south-east. The colonia would be settled by time-expired legionaries. Its official name was Colonia Claudia Victricensis and it is said to be located on the old legionary fortress. The colony was deliberately planned for these veterans, and did not follow the normal procedure of replanning an existing settlement. It was also normal practice at this time for a colonia to be surrounded by an area of land that could be divided up among the veterans so that they could establish themselves, and use the land as smallholdings.

According to Tacitus, the reasons for establishing a colonia at Camulodunum was to show to the Trinovantes, by example, how the Roman civilian lived. At the same time it was to provide on site a trained fighting reserve should the need arise. As a result Camulodunum was graced right from the start with magnificent public buildings and all the essential amenities of Roman town life. Theatres and baths were quickly erected, and Tacitus recorded that the town was renowned for its comforts, rather than as an area of protection.

All these amenities cost land and money, and the Trinovantes had to bear the brunt of heavy taxes. They also lost the use of land. Some experts think this was done by a continual process of acquisition and not outright in one go. Manpower would be needed for building the structures and making the fixtures and fittings to embellish them. After the expensive public buildings were finished they still had to be maintained and the ceremonies paid for, so there would be an on going levy imposed. Another factor which must have rankled with the Trinovantes was the harsh treatment they received from the Romans. This was in contrast to that of their neighbours, the Catuvellauni, who were allowed to keep their land and were granted other favours.

One of the major constructions in Camulodunum, and one that threw a huge burden on the Trinovantes in the form of taxes both during erection and afterwards, was the Temple of Claudius in the Forum - a wide piazza.

The platform on which the superstructure of this classical temple rested was built over four sand-filled vaults and measured 24 m x 32 m on foundations sunk 4 m deep. According to the experts this is larger than the normal classical temple found in provincial towns. Over 1000 years later the Normans were to make use of these foundations and erected their keep around the massive base. The remains can be still seen beneath the present day castle.

Rosalind Dunnett says 'the surviving podium is almost certainly the original first-century work, since being fireproof it would have survived the Boudiccan revolt. Very little, however, is known about the super-structure of this building or of its successor in the post-Boudiccan period. The upper surface of the podium stood over 3 m above the Roman ground level and must have been approached by a flight of steps in the classical tradition, and indeed the entire superstructure presumably conformed to the classical design of cella, peristyle and tri-angular roof. The upper surface of the podium was built of fine white mortar with a bonding course of tile. This probably provided a base for a stone or marble floor, but the original Roman surface was torn out, either in late Roman or in Norman times; none of the floor remains.'

As stated above, little is known of the superstructure of the building. However, in M R Hull's *Roman Colchester* the temple is described as being 'of a well-known classical style, with a deep portico eight columns wide and four deep. Colonnades ran along each side, but only half-engaged columns across the back. This plan is almost the same as that of the Temple of Mars Ultor in the Forum at Rome.'

At about this time loans were being called in, tax-gathers were busy extorting money to pay for the civic buildings. Labour would be required to produce the components and assemble the constructions. Land would be needed - not only for the buildings to stand on but for smallholdings for the colonists. It has been estimated that at least 500 km would have been required and this could only be forcibly appropriated from the Trinovantes. Greed certainly appeared to be a growing part of Roman rule in dealing with the local population.

The colonists' treatment of the Trinovantes left a lot to be desired. The natives found that they had lost their capital town of Colchester to the Romans and instead were offered land several miles away at Chelmsford, which was not at all to their liking. Tacitus wrote that 'the veterans were the especial object of their hatred. These men, recently settled at Camulodunum, had been turning them out of their homes, taking away their lands, and calling them prisoners and slaves.'

While all this was going on the military authorities looked the other way, and did nothing to check the behaviour of the veterans. Being men from the same mould they were probably hoping for similar licence when their turn came.

The moderate treatment given to the western neighbours, the Catuvellauni, is in complete contrast. Written sources give no indications of a harsh approach in the handling of this tribe. It does not appear to have been deprived of any land - in fact its canton was among the largest in Britain at that time - and it had the distinction of a municipium, or self government, at Verulamium. Certainly all this 'favouritism' added to the bitterness existing between the two tribes.

With the adjacent Iceni to the north feeling aggrieved, the Trinovantes appeared to have an ally. Over many years the two tribes were probably discussing among themselves the evils of occupation under the Romans, to compare their grievances, plan ways of settling old scores, and generally making life a little easier.

Eventually, during the summer of AD 60, the occasion for an uprising arrived. The king of the Iceni, Prasutagus, had died after a long and prosperous reign. He left his two daughters, together with Nero, the Roman Emperor, as co-heirs, in the misguided hope that with such subservience the kingdom, and his own property, would remain inviolate. His hopes were not to be realised; Nero's typical attitude to a half-share of an estate was that it showed ingratitude and, as a result, he usually ended up taking all of it. Added to this injury to the tribe's pride was the arrogance of the officers sent to safeguard the inheritance on the emperor's behalf - possibly matched by equal arrogance and inflexibility by the royal household.

As so often happens in times of death, both Prasutagus's property and kingdom were plundered. The kingdom by centurions and his household property by the procurator's slaves.

Worse still, his widow, Boudicca, was flogged and both his daughters raped; the king's relatives were treated like household slaves and the Iceni nobles were dispossessed of their ancestral estates, as though their lands were part of the will.

Inflamed by these outrages, and the thought of possibly more to follow, led to the Iceni taking up arms in a general uprising. In this they were joined by the Trinovantes. The two tribes must have been planning something for sometime, for as soon as the Roman governor, Suetonius Paulinus, was away leading a campaign in north Wales against the island of Mona [Anglesey], the Trinovantes and Iceni set out for revenge. The governor had taken most of the legionaries, leaving only a skeleton force between the Wash and the Thames to protect the south east.

In the words of Tacitus, 'With the governor away, the fears of the Britons had been removed, and they began to discuss among themselves the evils of slavery, to compare grievances, and to incite each other by the construction they placed upon them. Nothing, they argued, would be gained by patience... Under the leadership of Boudicca - for they do not discriminate against women in the matter of military command - they pursued the troops who were dispersed among the smaller forts, overwhelmed the camps, and then stormed the colony itself, as the very seat of slavery. Their barbarous anger in the hour of victory shrank from no form of atrocity,' He goes on to say that if Suetonius had not come to the rescue Britain would have been lost.

He continued that the Temple of Claudius seemed to have been established as the very citadel of enduring slavery, and its chosen priests, under the guise of a religious cult, were squandering the wealth of the whole country. To attack a position undefended by fortifications seemed no arduous undertaking; indeed, the Roman governors had scandalously neglected to take precautions, putting amenities before the needs of defence.

The colonia at Colchester, which 11 years after its foundation still had inadequate defences, was a major objective for the rebels. While on their way south, Boudicca and her followers achieved their first victory with an ambush on the IX legion. These troops, under the command of Petilius Cerealis, had been despatched to intercept the rebels as soon as the news of the revolt reached its Lincoln bases. Altogether 2,000 of his men - roughly a third of his force - were slaughtered. Cerealis and the cavalry made their escape.

Fired with this success the revolutionaries destroyed anything to do with the Romans that lay in their path. The workshop area in Sheepen was demolished, the old native dwelling site was reoccupied and its defences reinforced with a palisade, closely following the Sheepen dyke.

The veterans meanwhile had sent to the procurator, Catus Decianus, in London for help. He sent 200 men without proper equipment to strengthen the small garrison already in the area, and it is reported that they were all killed.

The rebels then turned their attention to the colonia which was looted and burned to the ground. Archaeologists have found evidence of this wide scale desolation over the whole area covered by the colonia, and so far no building has yet been discovered that escaped destruction by fire. Anyone wanting more information about the archæological discoveries of this period will find Rosalind Dunnett's *The Trinovantes* helpful, and it points out that, with all the large scale slaughter that took place, only one skeleton has been found that can be directly related to the revolution.

Those fortunate enough to escape from the colonia sort refuge in the Temple. They barricaded themselves in and withstood the attack for two days and two nights. Eventually they were overrun, and the resulting slaughter was truly horrendous. Bursting in, the insurgents put to death by sword and torture men and women alike. It is reported by Tacitus that over 70,000 Roman citizens and allies were massacred in Colchester, London and St Albans.

It is hard to understand why the Romans did nothing to maintain or strengthen their defences before the revolt, or even once it had started. They had time to send for reinforcements and omens abounded on a large scale, according to Tacitus. He wrote that, for no apparent reason, the statue of Victory at Camulodunum fell down, its back turned as though yielding to an enemy. Frenzied women prophesied destruction, saying that barbarian yells had been heard in the senate house, the theatre had echoed with the howling of wild beasts, and a vision of a phantom colony had been seen in the Thames estuary, sacked and destroyed: nay, the very ocean reeked of blood, and the ebbing tide left an imprint of corpses on the shore.

Led by Boudicca, the horde then advanced on Londinium, with a possible diversion to a settlement at Chelmsford. Excavations in the Chelmsford area revealed that a masonry bath house was destroyed by fire at about this time. Tacitus does make the point though that during her march on London Boudicca stayed away from any forts on route, so it would appear that there was no fort at Chelmsford at this time.

On reaching London, inhabitants that remained in the town were butchered by the rebels and the place plundered. They then marched on to Verulamium which suffered the same fate.

The Britons took no prisoners, their only thoughts were of slaughter, the gibbet, fire and the cross.

Suetonius force marched from Anglesey, possibly with only his cavalry, and caught the rebel hordes at London. On the way he summoned the II Augusta from the Gloucester region. For various reasons, among them the town's lack of troops, Suetonius decided to leave London to its fate. Incidentally, the commander of the II Augusta, Poenius Postmus, refused to obey orders and did not join Suetonius.

When a battle eventually took place Suetonius wanted it to be on his terms, at a location where the enemy was only in front, and where there was no cover for ambush. A massive battle did take place at an unknown spot. Some experts believe it was along Watling Street, somewhere between Towcester and Atherstone. Suetonius had the XIV Legion, a detachment of the XX and many auxiliary troops, altogether around 10,000 men.

'Never had they massed in such great numbers' is how Tacitus described the Britons, who were so confident of victory that they had brought along their families. They suffered terrible defeat when they became entangled with their own baggage line. The defeat became a massacre as the Romans took their revenge. One report put the rebel deaths at 80,000 and the Romans at only 400. A number of insurgents must have escaped as Tacitus hints of raids continuing for several months more. Boudicca is said to have ended her life with poison. Once news of this event spread any further resistance must have collapsed rapidly. When the commander of the II Augusta, Poenius Postmus, heard of the victory he fell on his sword for his defiance.

Treatment of the rebels after this defeat was very severe. Work was put in hand to strengthen the military establishments. A fort was erected at Chelmsford, and the construction of a large fort situated at Great Chesterford was started.

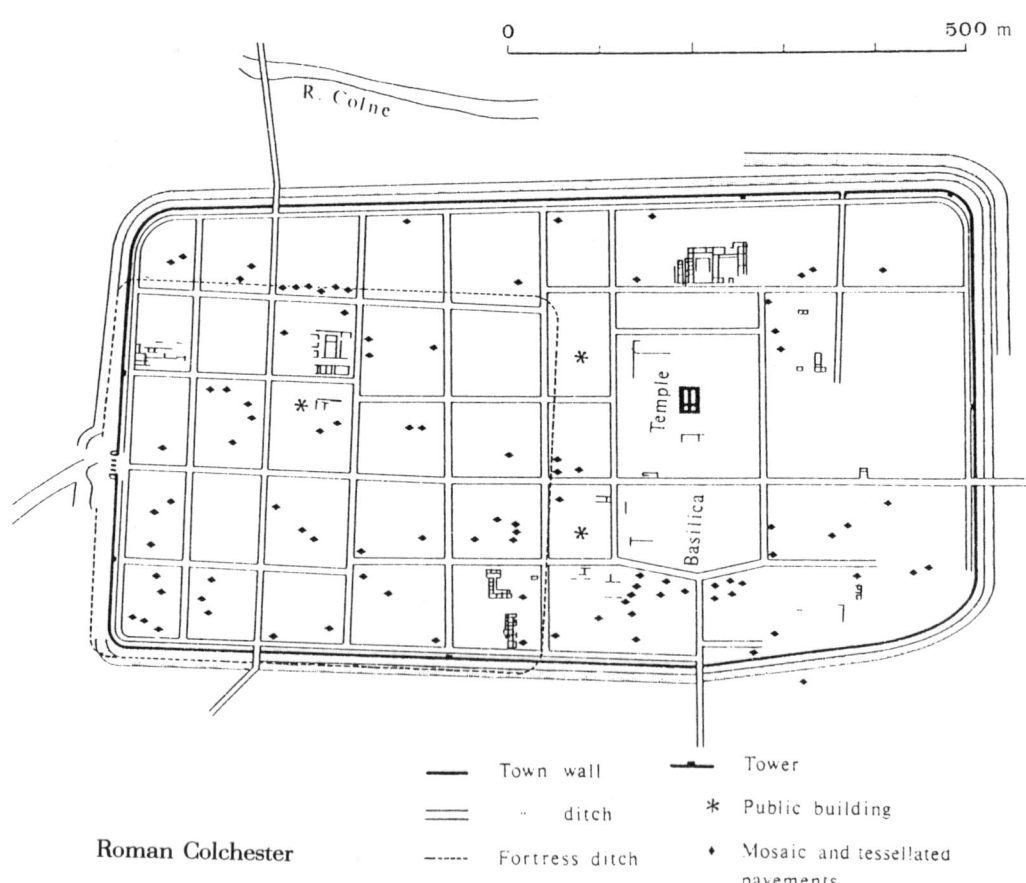

Roman Colchester

—— Town wall	▬ Tower
══ " ditch	* Public building
----- Fortress ditch	✦ Mosaic and tessellated pavements

Chapter 4
The Count of the Saxon Shore

Once the uprising was contained and peace was again restored, life gradually returned to normal, although the treatment meted out to the rebels was initially very harsh. Following the revolution any reference to the Trinovantes disappears from historical records. Did the tribe survive? Was the tribe dispersed together with its territory among its neighbours? According to Tacitus this was unlikely as appeasement was the name of the game, and there was no reason why the Trinovantes should receive worse treatment than the Iceni who, although heavily taxed for a number of generations, still retained its tribal identity.

About this period defences in the form of ditches were provided around Colchester. Their usefulness, however, was short lived as recent excavations have shown that they were deliberately filled in after a very brief period. As Tacitus's writings indicate that the town had no protection at the time of the uprising it would appear that these ditches were dug after the revolution.

Slowly Colchester recovered and by the end of the first century prosperity appeared on the scene for both the colonies and its surrounding area. Shortly afterwards, during the Hadrianic period, Colchester was allowed to enclose an area of 108 acres with a fine masonry wall with imposing gateways, although there was no military necessity for defences at this time. The work it seems was only finished on the west side, the rest was left incomplete.

Experts conclude that Colchester's town wall was erected some time before the third century when most of the Roman town walls were built in Britain. They date it around the middle of the second century. Again the wall differs from the normal style of the period in that it was free-standing; the rampart behind it was built a number of years later.

Analysis shows the rampart to be composed of domestic debris and rubbish from wattle and daub houses rather than the traditional material excavated by digging a town ditch. Despite vandalism over the years by later generations using the wall as a handy supply of stone and brick for building operations, there remains today a considerable length providing an impressive illustration of Roman military engineering. It was dominated on the western side by the Balkerne Gate, said to be the largest at the time in Britain, protecting the major road leading to London. The gate is described as a quadruple structure having a double carriageway and two pedestrian ways which were flanked by quadrant-shaped guard rooms.

Around the wall altogether there were said to be six gates. The East Gate survived until the seventeenth century with most of it collapsing in 1651, three years after the Civil War reached Colchester. So it is possible the siege helped in its demise.

At around the same period indications are that the fort at Chelmsford was rebuilt. The defences at Chelmsford took the form of a ditch and bank, but were not maintained for very long. A large fort was established at Great Chesterford, which being at the junction of three Roman roads, was considered of major military importance. The fort occupied about 35 acres (14 ha) and housed half a legion together with various auxiliary troops. It was not until the fourth century that Great Chesterford was considered to be important enough for a town wall and ditch.

The years between 213 and 342 AD have been described as 'years of peace', but during the whole of that period a continual threat existed from the sea as well as the land. In the north of the country the Romans were having problems with attacks from over Hadrian's Wall, and with attacks from over the sea from Ireland. In the southeastern part of Britain cruel and merciless pirates descended on undefended parts of the coast in their boats and carried off the property of wealthy Romans, as well as men and women for slaves. These pirates were the Saxons, who later became the conquerors and settlers of England. They were confirmed enemies of the Romans. Their homeland was in the vicinity of Jutland, and they were said to be as fierce and barbaric as the attackers in the north, but were better equipped and armed. At first they may only have attacked local shipping and the coastal trade, but gradually as their confidence grew so they began assaulting exposed colonies.

To be able to destroy the pirates on their home territory, the Romans would require a good fleet of ships, and this was one area where the Romans were weak. Additionally, it was the duty of the Emperor to see that the frontier was safely protected, not something the inhabitants should do themselves. So with no navy and the protection of the country the responsibility of an officer who was residing on the continent, defence was limited to the erection of forts.

By the fourth century the situation became so desperate that at any suitable point on the coast between the Wash and Beachy Head, where an inlet of the sea afforded an entry to the pirates, fortresses were built. In an effort to deal with the pirate attacks on the eastern coast two large Roman coastal forts were built to protect the inlets. One was built at Othona, which is thought to be the name for Bradwell-on-Sea, and the other at Walton Castle, Suffolk. They were part of a much larger defensive system, known as the Forts of the Saxon Shore, extending from Branchester in Norfolk around to Portchester Castle on the south coast near Portsmouth.

Bradwell fort lies on the exposed, low-lying south bank of the Blackwater river with no marshland to intervene and commands a fine view out to sea. Today, all that remains are the unimpressive foundations unearthed in 1864 with the building of the seawall. It is more than likely that some of the stone from the fort was used to construct the nearby chapel of St Peter-on-the-Wall, some time between 653 and 664. The chapel is thought to be built across the main entrance at the western end

St Peter ad Murum and
the layout of Othona

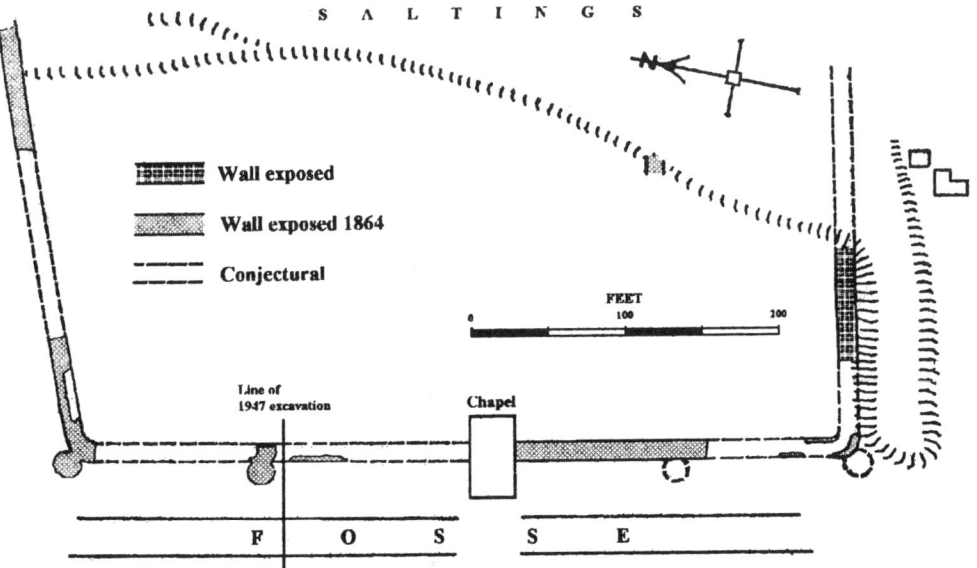

S A L T I N G S

Wall exposed

Wall exposed 1864

Conjectural

FEET

0   100   200

Line of
1947 excavation

Chapel

F   O   S   S   E

of the fort. Work in 1865 revealed the line of the surviving fort wall. The 12 ft (4.2 m) thick walls nearly form a square enclosure with rounded corners, and at the north-west corner were solid, horseshoe shaped fortifications. Its width was 157 m, but the length is unknown due to the eastern end extending into the marsh-land.

Additional protection was provided about 40 ft (12 m) outside the wall on the west and north sides by a 25 ft (8 m) moat, or fosse.

The guide to the fort and chapel tells us that 'no masonry is visible above the surface except for a section of wall on the south side... Here a characteristic alternation of four courses of stone with three of bonding tile can be seen, with an offset of tile at the foot to bring the wall out to the concrete foundations. The ditch here is wide and deep and comes up almost to the wall, unlike the ditch on the west side. The eastern front must have been occupied by a quay, like that at Portchester.

There is no trace of a gate where one would expect it, facing the road inland. It is therefore naturally assumed that the chapel covers its foundation. There was probably a postern-gate in the north wall.'

The officer in charge was known as the Count of the Saxon Shore (*Comes Littoris Saxonici*) and one of the first was Carausius. He came from the Low Countries and entered Roman service where he exhibited great amphibious skills as a commander. One school of thought suggests that he built the circle of forts around the coast with a view to preventing Roman attacks rather than piratical raids. He had been accused of letting a raid take place and then on its return journey relieving it of its spoil. As a result he had been condemned to death by Emperor Maximian. To escape he sailed with his fleet to Britain, where the Roman garrisons joined him. For seven years he succeeded in protecting his regions until 293 when he was killed by one of his officers. Later, when the Romans left Britain, the forts continued to defend the south-east coasts against the Saxon attacks.

As was their usual custom the Romans garrisoned most of these forts not with regular legionaries, but with auxiliaries recruited from various parts of the empire. Stationed at the fort of Othona, was a force of horsemen known as Fortenses whose homeland, Limem Fortensis, was in North Africa. Later on, during the fourth century, it is highly probable that local people were employed.

What is not known is how long the Othona fort was manned, or the part it played in the prolonged conflict between the Romano-Briton and the Anglo-Saxon. Neither is it known when the walls collapsed, but it must have been in a state of disrepair at the time the adjacent chapel was built for the stone to be used in the latter's construction. What is known from the Anglo-Saxon Chronicle was that a great tide occurred at Martinmas, 1099, which could also have affected the remains at that time.

Coastal erosion has left nothing of the other Saxon Shore fort on the east coast at Walton Castle, any details that are recorded were compiled around 1722. The eighteenth century description says the fort walls were built of stone with tile bonding courses. It ran parallel with the coast for about 295 ft (90 m) before turning sharply, which way is not recorded, Dr Knight, the recorder, notes several remains of buildings uncovered at low water, but these could result from the castle built in the twelfth century. An inconclusive plan drawing of the fort made in 1623 shows a stone wall with projecting corner fortifications like those at Bradwell, but leaves many questions unanswered.

During the decade beginning 360 AD the Picts from north of the border, the Scots from Ireland, the Attacoti, probably from north of the border and the Saxons increased the frequency of their raids. No part of the country was secure and the east coast suffered as badly as the rest. The army was in no state to repel these attacks as troops had been withdrawn to defend Rome, and the British garrisons were left below strength.

The raids culminated in the barbarian plot of 367 AD when all the protagonists combined to assail the whole country. What effect this had on the Essex area is hard to say as archæologists have unearthed very little evidence of the disaster. For example, the remains at Bradwell show no indication of conflict. It is known that the Count of the Saxon Shore was killed during the conflict.

During this period Britain was defended by what is called a field army, and it can be identified by the characteristic belt fittings its soldiers wore. Some of these have been found around the county at Mucking, Colchester, Great Chesterford, Bradwell fort, Gestingthorpe, Kelvedon and Rivenhall.

This riotous state of affairs lasted for a couple of years before the emperor Valentinian sent four regiments under the command of Count Theodosius to restore order to the province. He set about reconstructing the defences of places such as Bradwell, but the finds indicate the villas in the Trinovantian canton, such as Gestingthorpe and Ixworth, as well as towns, were afforded protection by soldiers. The type of military equipment unearthed, mainly consisting of chip-carved bronze belt fittings and buckles, shows that Germanic mercenaries were stationed in these areas.

Colchester's defences were improved and it appears that around the late fourth century 14 ha of Great Chesterford was surrounded by an impressive town wall and ditch. There was no way the town itself could pay for these elaborate fortifications, so for some reason assistance must have been provided.

Over the years the raids by the marauders continued to grow. In the middle of the fourth century Germanic mercenaries, or farmer-warriors, were brought in to support the area's depleted defences, as archæological excavations at Mucking have revealed. By the first half of the fifth century, when the Romans withdrew to defend their homeland from Gothic attacks, the barbarians were being settled in the exposed districts to defend the countryside as well as the towns. At about this period, large areas of land in the south east must have passed out of Trinovantian hands. As the century progressed new immigrants continually augmented the number of Germanic early settlers.

Evidence is growing from excavations that a slow and peaceful influx of Saxons and a gradual collapse of the Romano-British way of life was taking place. There is a singular lack of evidence of destruction or violence.

It was around the time of the departure of the Romans and the arrival of the Saxons seizing the low coastal land to the north of the Thames that Essex received its name as the home of the 'East Saxons'. The term English also appeared at about the same time, relating to the people living in East Anglia.

However, this peaceful situation did not last long and gradually the mercenaries attitude changed from 'service' to aggression. Immigration continued with more and more Saxons arriving and settling initially in the south east area of the country. What has become clear over the years is that Essex, in particular, was able to successfully resist indiscriminate barbaric attacks during the fifth and sixth centuries which engulfed the rest of eastern and nearly the whole of southern Britain.

This is not to say that the East Saxons were not involved with sporadic fighting. In the west country in 552, the West Saxon King, Cynric, became master of Salisbury Plain when he stormed the divided Britons and captured Sorbiounum (Old Sarum). He then continued to fight his way to the Thames valley where he turned eastward in an endeavour to reach the estuary. His plans were thwarted by the East Saxons who had anticipated his moves and attacked and captured London where a number of them settled. They became known as the 'Middle Saxons' and gave their name to Middlesex.

Gradually a more settled way of life descended on the population, and for a while the average Saxon was less likely to meet a sudden violent end to his life than at any period previously. All that came to an end about 835 when the Vikings (adventurers from Scandinavia) attacked the Isle of Sheppey on the other side of the Thames. Thus began another unsettled period which was to continue for the next 30 years.

Chapter 5
The coming of the Vikings

There was a slight chance of a united England around the year 659, which was very quickly dashed. Three large kingdoms existed - North-humberland, Wessex and Mercia - and were to do so for at least another hundred and fifty years. Also there were four smaller kingdoms - Essex, East Anglia, Sussex and Kent - who usually sided with either Wessex or Mercia.

Occasionally a strong king came to the fore, like Æthelbald, king of the Mercians, who, while disturbances were causing distractions in the west country, took the opportunity to invade Wessex and make himself master of the country, and overlord of all the kingdoms south of the Humber. In 754 the West Saxons rebelled and at Burford defeated him.

Offa, who succeeded Æthelbald, after a few years once again attempted the long and difficult task of bringing the whole of southern England under his rule. In 775, after a long and bitter struggle he finally brought both Kent and Essex (whose King then was Swithred) under his domination.

For most of this period there does not appear to have been much work carried out to fortify sites, most of the battles being fought on open spaces. As most of the major fights took place away from the county, there have not been any Saxon defences uncovered in Essex dated before 913.

Eventually the common enemy came from outside these shores from the north, from Denmark and Norway. These invaders resembled the ferocious warriors of three and four centuries earlier, the Angles and Saxons. Christianity had taken over as a religion in most parts of England, while the 'religion' of the raiders swarming over the seas was the old one of force. They plundered the stored-up wealth wherever they could find it along the coasts of Western Europe. The first raids on this country started around the year 787.

The Vikings and Norsemen loved battle, possibly more than plunder, and believed that any warrior killed in battle was taken to Valhalla where they were received by the god Odin. Once there these immortal heroes would spend their days fighting and hacking one another to pieces. At the end of the day their wounds would be healed, there would be feasting and revelry and on the following day the activity would begin again. Those unfortunate to die in bed went to the dwelling of the goddess Hela, the Norse equivalent of Hell.

In the years since the Angles and Saxons first began raiding the country, the settlers had lost the skills of seamanship. Therefore, unless the attacking Northmen could be detained and fought on land they were free to take what they wanted and sail away unmolested. By the time the local ruler, or ealdorman, could gather his own warriors, the fyrd, or levy of all the male population of fighting age, and converge on the coastal area being plundered, the raiders were well out to sea. As their courage increased so the Northmen raided further and further from their boats, offering better opportunities for the local inhabitants to attack the marauders.

Raids became more persistent. In the reign of Ethelwulf the attacks spread over the whole of the eastern and southern coasts, with the pirates staying ashore long enough to fight a number of pitched battles. These resulted in the raiders feeling strong enough to stay, culminating in the episode when around 350 ships beached in the mouth of the Thames and the crews sacked both London and Canterbury, before deciding to stay in Thanet the whole winter of 851.

Later the Vikings came not to plunder the countryside but to settle as conquerors. They overran North-humberland and overcame the resistance of the East Anglians. During this episode the king, Eadmund, was fastened to a tree and shot dead with arrows, then his head was cut off. His subjects, who saw him as a saint, were determined to erect a worthwhile shrine in his honour. Later it was transformed into a large monastery at Beodoricsworth (later Bury St Edmunds) and his body transferred there.

So turbulent was this period as the Vikings launched devastating attack after attack around the coast and beyond, some experts suggest that the English nation was in danger of annihilation.

Ælfred, famous for burning the cakes, became king in 871 and also became the saviour of the nation. He had to resort to guerrilla warfare against the Danes. During 878 he defeated the Danish king, Guthrum, which resulted in the Treaty of Wedmore in 885/6, after further hostilities. Under this treaty Ælfred kept Wessex, with its dependencies, Kent and Sussex and the western part of Mercia. The rest of England up to and including the Tees, Essex, together with all the land east of Watling Street, belonged to the Danes and later came to be known as the Danelaw - as the law was Danish and not Saxon. In the 13 years leading up to the Treaty, it appears that no land or sea battle took place involving Essex in any way.

More successes in 886 resulted in the handing over of London and its surrounding districts to Ælfred. Further invasions by the Vikings eventually brought Ælfred and his army into Essex.

After being driven from Rochester in Kent in 884, Guthrum's Danes were attacked by Ælfred's fleet off East Anglia. The sea-fight in the mouth of the Stour, is the first known battle directly connected with the county. It resulted in 16 Danish ships being captured and their crews killed. Unfortunately the victors, in their turn, were shortly defeated by a superior force.

After ravaging the continent in 893 the Danish army crossed the Channel from France and returned to its camp which had recently been constructed at Benfleet. The following year their leader, Haesten, unwisely set out on a plundering raid to Mercia at the same time as Ælfred swept down from London to Benfleet with a large force comprised of militia from London and the West Saxons. He attacked

Benfleet and took the stronghold. He captured Haesten's wife and two sons, who were later released. Haesten then retired to Shoebury where he set about repairing and fortifying the camp earthworks.

Confirmation of this dramatic action is recorded in the Anglo-Saxon Chronicle 'With the citizens and the help which came to them from the west, they went east to Benfleet... Haesten had made that fort at Benfleet before this, and was then off on a plundering raid while the great host was in occupation. Then the English advanced, and put that host to flight, stormed the fort, and seized everything inside it, both property and women and also children, and conveyed them all to London: and all the ships they either broke up and burned up or brought to London or to Rochester. And Haesten's wife and his two sons were brought to the king, and he restored them to Haesten because one of them was his godson and the other was the godson of ealdorman Ethelred.'

At South Benfleet no trace of the Danish earthworks can be found. The site is believed to be in the area of the present churchyard and enclosed to the west and north by the Benfleet Creek backwater. Remains of burnt ships and skeletons unearthed when the railway bridge over the backwater was built in 1855 were thought to have been relics from this period when Ælfred defeated the Vikings. Most experts believe the camp was located in the vicinity of the church.

Although occupied for a relatively short period the redoubtable stronghold at Shoebury was located near the seashore. It was bounded on the north eastern side by what is now Rampart Street and Artillery Barracks has been built over the Såxon camp. There was originally a 70 yard rampart with evidence of an external ditch travelling from Smith Street in a south western direction. Measurements of the ditch are said to be 40 ft (1 2m) wide and 9 ft (2.7 m) deep.

This site was the base for launching a raid to the Severn valley. A second foray to Chester and Wales was unsuccessful as a scorched earth policy adopted by the defenders meant a return to Essex and a temporary camp at Mersea Island for Haesten.

The following year, 895, saw Haesten's forces leave their temporary camp at Mersea and take what was left of their ships up the Thames. Even on this expedition Haesten's luck seems to have deserted him as yet again he was beaten and scattered.

At the time of his death in 899 Ælfred had fortified London and was able to leave his son, Eadward the Elder, a small, strong and consolidated kingdom. Eadward's reign began with opposition from Ælfred's nephew, Æthelwald, who - driven to the north - was busy in Danish Northumbria in 901 preparing for an invasion of the south. Putting the plan into action the following year he sailed down to Essex and, on landing, accepted the surrender of the people.

There then ensued a series of running battles between the two sides with the Essex men siding with Æthelwald, which culminated in the battle fought on the river Holme in 903. Although the Danes held on, this fight to the finish produced so many casualties on both sides that a temporary truce brought a halt to the current hostilities.

A major consideration of Eadward's over the next three years was how to win back the land from the Danes and recreate a unified kingdom that had been his father's dream. For a start he built a 'burh', or fortified enclosure, at Hertford in 912. The following year he erected another at Witham, while his army was camped at Maldon. As he advanced and secured each district so he built another burh.

Archaeological excavations to prove the plan and location of the two Essex burhs have been indecisive and there is still much to be established. At Maldon a description was published in 1775 by Joseph Strutt and Nathaniel Salmon which positions the squarish enclave on the western side of the town bisected by the London Road. Strutt produced two sketches of the burh, with one illustrating a plan view of rough ground and a quadrangle with the corners rounded.

Over the next four years the Danes continued to harass Eadward with a series of hit and run raids before retiring for a while. Eadward continued his programme of building burh across the country and in 916 established one at Maldon. It was these fortified positions which turned the tide of success in Eadward's favour. Once the Danes realised this their objective became the capture of these important posts.

Still taking the initiative, Eadward called more men to arms, led them to Colchester and took the town. The Danes' reply was to sail down the coast to attack Maldon in an endeavour to cut his supply links between London and Colchester. But the defenders held out and, with reinforcements, counter-attacked to scatter the enemy. Eadward gained more territory and consolidated his defences by repairing the damaged Roman town wall at Colchester. Eadward's campaigns continued and the Danes were contained over the remaining six years of his life. He died in 925.

Eadward's eldest son, Athelstan, picked up the work started by his grandfather, and continued by his father, of endeavouring to unify the country. He won a famous battle in 937 by beating the Norsemen at Brunanburh in Northumbria. To establish a national feeling throughout the territory under his command he developed towns based on the martial burhs, such as Colchester, Maldon and Witham, and by encouraging trade.

Athelstan died in 940 and was succeeded by his brother Eadmund. Eadmund secured an alliance with Malcolm, king of the Scots, to make the dominant powers in these islands English and Scots, leaving the Danes as a minor influence. An outlaw killed Eadmund while he was at a feast in his hall in 946, and Eadward's youngest son, Eadred, became king. Eadred succeeded in completing what Ælfred had started. These achievements were not to last and from 955 the country began falling apart.

Under Æthelred the Redeless, or the man without counsel, better known as the Unready, things really began to disintegrate. He was considered to be a man without kingly qualities and his reign of 38 years is remembered for incompetence and treachery.

By 984 the Norsemen were once again plundering the country and taking off with their booty. They were finding the defenceless communities along the coast easy picking, and would dash in, murdering, stealing and burning before departing loaded down with spoil. Unlike the raiders in the time of Ælfred, who were migrating warrior farmers looking for land on which to settle, these invaders were ferocious professional fighters owing loyalty to no one but themselves.

At the time of the 991 Viking landings in East Anglia, first at Ipswich followed by Maldon, Byrhtnoth, like so many other leaders in the future, was in the north demonstrating his powers of leadership. As soon as the news of the invasion reached him he headed south and hurried to protect his home in Hadleigh, Suffolk. Byrhtnoth was a tall man, well over six feet, and in his sixties. (His grave in Ely Cathedral was opened during restoration work in 1769, the thigh bone was measured and it was deduced that Byrhtnoth stood 6 ft 9 in. tall.) He was recognised as a true servant of the Crown and benefactor of the church. He was originally a thane and now was ealdorman of Essex (ealdorman - a royal official often acting as the king's deputy), whose authority included Huntingdon and Cambridge as well as Essex. Being a very experienced general Byrhtnoth most probably guessed that the Danes would eventually head for Maldon. Circumstances dictated that for this battle he took the title of Leader of the English.

The events of the battle and the slaying of Byrhtnoth are briefly recorded in four of the versions of the Anglo-Saxon Chronicle (versions C, D, E and F). This historical record was started on the orders of Ælfred and is said to be the earliest history which any European nation possesses in its own tongue. The E version for 991 says 'In this year Ipswich was harried and very soon afterwards Ealdorman Byrhtnoth was slain at Maldon. In this year it was decided for the first time to pay tribute to the Danes because of the great terror they inspired along the sea coast. On this first occasion it amounted to £10,000. This course was adopted on the advice of Archbishop [of Canterbury (990-994)] Sigeric.'

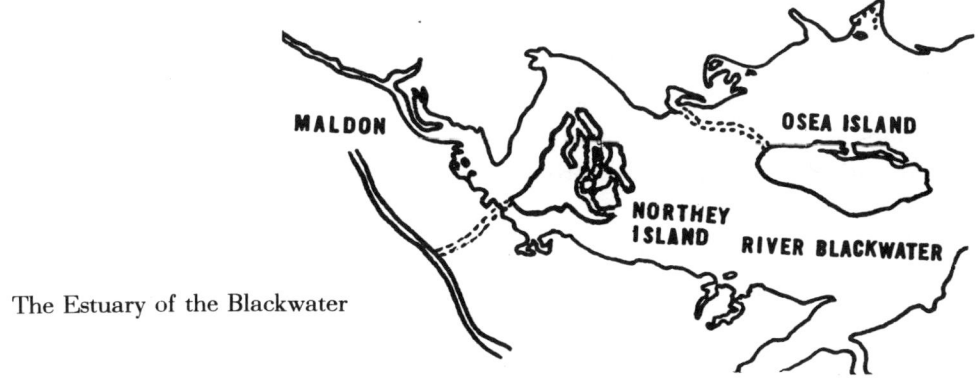

The Estuary of the Blackwater

Chapter 6
The battles of Maldon and Ashingdon

Until 975 England had had a navy of around 3,600 ships, organised in three fleets. Each year just after Easter they would set sail and patrol the coasts of Britain making it very difficult for raiders to slip through. However, between 979 and 988, during the reign of Æthelred the Unready, the navy must have become disorganised as the Danes commenced invading the eastern shores again.

In 991, 93 ships carrying a large army under the command of Olaf Trygvason, later King of Norway, battered the Kent coast before heading north to sack Ipswich and the surrounding area. Boosted by this success some of the ships sailed south and up the River Panta, now the Blackwater, to land on Northey Island prior to attacking Maldon.

In the meantime Byrhtnoth had arrived home from the north and began trying to gather the fyrd - the name for the military force and the obligation to serve; it was one of the three duties of the thegns - but the Essex men did not want to know, perhaps because it was harvest time. However, he assembled a relatively small, highly skilled, well equipped band of warriors and led them to Maldon, and the causeway from the mainland to Northey Island.

On the morning of 10 August, 991, Byrhtnoth was ready to defend his homeland, and being on the mainland he had the advantage. According to the poem after riding about reminding his warriors how they should behave in battle, Byrhtnoth dismounted and took his place among his men. A Viking appeared to offer peace in exchange for gold, terms which were quickly refused with much shaking of spear and shield. Then Byrhtnoth advanced his troops to the river bank.

To start with the two sides could only stare, yell and fire arrows at each other, as the tide kept them apart. As it began to ebb the causeway appeared and the Vikings began to wade across. Byrhtnoth ordered Wulfstan, son of Ceola, to defend the causeway, and he 'with his spear fatally shot the first man who very rashly stepped on to the causeway'. Two other proven warriors, Elfere and Maccus stood with Wulfstan, and nothing could have forced them to take flight as long as they were able to wield their weapons.

When the Vikings realised this they asked permission to cross. 'Then,' says the poem, 'in foolhardy pride the earl allowed those hateful people access to the ford.' The Danes crossed over and battle was joined. 'The clamour began; the ravens wheeled and the eagle circled overhead, craving for carrion, there was shouting on earth'.

The battle raged for many hours with first one side then the other gaining the upper hand.

Finally the earl was wounded by a spear which broke when he hit it with his shield and it came out. Byrhtnoth advanced on his attacker and with his spear killed him, stabbing him first through the throat and then through the heart.

A second javelin pierced Byrhtnoth, this time fatally. A young English warrior, Wulfinaer, son of Wulfstan, pulled it out and returned it with full force, and accuracy, at the original Viking thrower who dropped to the ground dead. Byrhtnoth drew his sword and as other seafarers attacked him, he was hit on the arm, his sword dropped away and he was left defenceless.

The translation of the poem in *The Anglo-Saxon World - an anthology* says:-

> Then a seafarer bore down on the earl,
> he had it in mind to snatch away his treasures -
> his armour and rings and ornamented sword.
> Byrhtnoth drew out his sword from its sheath,
> broad-faced and gleaming, and slashed at his corselet,
> but one of the seafarers stopped him all too soon,
> he destroyed the earl Byrhtnoth's arm.
> The golden-hilted sword dropped from his hand.
> He could hold it no longer, nor wield
> a weapon of any kind. Then still the old warrior
> spoke these words, encouraged the warriors,
> called on his brave companions to do battle again.'

His retainers, Walnoth and Wulfmaer, were killed and Byrhtnoth's head was cut off by the Vikings. Seeing their leader fall a number of the fyrdmen rapidly left the field. Among them, despite his boastful promises at council, was Godric, and his two brothers, Godwine and Godwig, on the ealdorman's horses. Byrhtnoth's body was later taken to Ely Cathedral for burial.

It was at this point that the young soldier, Elfwine, made his attempt to encourage his fellow thegns. Although the English continued to fight valiantly in the tradition expected of them, the Vikings eventually won the day, but at a tremendous cost.

The big question in this battle must be, why did Byrhtnoth allow the Vikings free access across the causeway, and throw away his big advantage? John McSween in his book *Byrhtnoth - Anglo-Saxon warrior* suggests that 'the ealdorman decided that by giving the raiders access to firmer ground the issue could be concluded in favour of the English... However, the most... compelling explanation... is provided by recent research into what might be called, the ritual of Battle.

'Early Saxon armies fought their battles according to a set of traditional rules. The combatants would decide the conflict on accepted battlefields, and certain ritualistic rules of engagement would be observed. In the case of Maldon it is plausible that the Vikings allowed Byrhtnoth time to assemble his army, and he was therefore expected and obliged to make a similar gesture. Consequently, after the traditional demand for tribute had been made and refused, Byrhtnoth was required to give ground as part of the ritual. Although this may seem to be something of a romantic concept associated with the ideal of English fair play, it does have echoes in literature such as Malory's *Le Morte d'Arthur*, and, more importantly, *Beowulf*.

For the local inhabitants they at least were spared ransacking and death as Byrhtnoth's tremendous fight had prevented complete destruction of the countryside. The king and his council thought otherwise. Their decision was to pay the Vikings £10,000 to abstain from plundering. Unfortunately, this payment of Danegeld had the opposite effect, and the Vikings only came back for ever-increasing amounts.

In 994 two men who had been driven from kingship, Olaf Trygvason of Norway, and Swein of Denmark, joined forces to attack London where the citizens successfully fought them off. The two chieftains and their army then turned to harrying, burning and slaying the surrounding counties of Essex, Kent, Sussex and Hampshire. Again, they were bought off by Æthelred paying them £16,000. Olaf sailed away, but Swein continued to make a nuisance of himself and had to be bought off yet again. By 1013 he controlled the Danish districts in the north and east, and Mercia and Wessex submitted to him to avoid being destroyed. In the meanwhile Æthelred fled to Normandy.

About this time, 1008 in fact, the forerunner of the ship money levy made its appearance, with the introduction of a law that every 310 hides of land should build and equip a warship.

In Essex a hide is approximately 120 acres - across the country as a whole the figure varies.

In 1014 Swein who was still in this country died at Gainsborough and his warriors elected Cnut (Canute), aged 21, as leader and king.

That same year Æthelred came back to England and was 'received with joy'. He died naturally on St George's Day two years later and his eldest son, Eadmund Ironside, succeeded him. By his vigour Eadmund attempted to restore the English kingship. At the time he received the crown Eadmund had already been battling it out with Cnut for three years with no successful conclusion as to who should rule England.

Another key player in this saga is the powerful Eadric Streona of Mercia, who has been described as 'a man of low birth, shrewd intellect, of an eloquent tongue, which he used only to persuade men to mischief'.

He decided to throw in his lot with the Danish king Cnut during the latter's siege of London in 1015. It was at this time that Eadmund Ironside was proclaimed king by the council in London and started to defeat the Vikings in battle. After a number of successes by Eadmund, Eadric of Mercia changed sides again and joined Eadmund at Aylesford. Why King Eadmund should accept the allegiance of Eadric is hard to understand, because according to the Anglo-Saxon Chronicle written by Florence of Worcester, 'No greater error of judgement was ever made than this'.

By the time these two great warriors met at Ashingdon they had already fought five battles in the space of six months, with Eadmund victorious each time. But they were indecisive in that they did not stop Danish plundering.

This time Cnut was on his way back to his ships, anchored in the Crouch, from a raid into southern Mercia, possibly the counties of Buckinghamshire and Oxfordshire. Eadmund, who had been recruiting in the West Country again called together his Army, ('all the English nation' the Anglo-Saxon Chronicle says with over-emphasis) set of after him. Cnut determined to safely install his loot on board his ships before being caught, hastily fell back. Eadmund, equally determined, gave chase and caught them not far from the Essex river landing site, on a down called Ashingdon. Eventually Cnut's troops were drawn up on the hill at Canewdon. In this position Cnut could not retreat any further without losing everything including his ships, so he was obliged to stand and fight. Eadmund's numerically superior forces were camped at Ashingdon. In these positions the two armies would be in full view of each other.

The resulting bloody and decisive battle took place on St Luke's Day, 18 October, 1016.

In the morning Eadmund assembled his men in three divisions and went round reminding them of their earlier victories and assuring them they could win again. At last he gave the signal to advance and give battle. We are told by Florence of Worcester that 'Eadmund moved his forces rapidly and fell suddenly on the enemy', while Cnut proceeded more cautiously and 'led his troops by slow march down to level ground.' Both armies fought well and large numbers of men fell on both sides, with the advantage appearing to favour the English. Then Eadric, who commanded the West Mercian troops, did as he had often done before, deserted to Cnut with the section he commanded. The fighting continued until the sun set (vespers?) when king Eadmund was able to withdraw from the battlefield with his much depleted army.

After fighting all day Cnut's troops were too exhausted to give chase.

The slaughter was terrible. No mention is made of the number killed, but Roger of Wendover records a list of those of high rank and mentions that almost all the English nobility fell. Florence of Worcester sums it up better with his 'and all the flower of England perished there'. According to the Latin poem *Encomium Emmae*, written nearly 20 years later to the honour of Cnut's queen Emma, the double-dealing of ealdorman Eadric had been agreed with Cnut sometime before the battle.

The report in the Anglo-Saxon Chronicle reads:

The host (Cnut's and his army of raiders) went back up into Essex, and made their way into Mercia, destroying everything before them. When the king (Eadmund Ironside) learnt that the host had appeared on the scene, then for the fifth time he called up all the people of England and followed them up, overtaking them in

Essex, at the hill called Ashingdon, and there a fierce battle was fought. Then ealdorman Eadric did as he had so often done before; he and the Magesaete (his supporters from Herefordshire and south Shropshire) were the first to set the example of flight, and thus he betrayed his royal lord and all the people of England. Cnut was victorious and won all England by his victory. Among the slain were bishop Eadnoth, abbot Wulfsige, ealdorman Ælfric, ealdorman Godwine, Ulfcytel from East Anglia, and Æthelweard, son of ealdorman Æthelwine, and all the oldest retainers in England.'

Although Eadmund was defeated, at a meeting between the two kings at Alney, near Deerhurst, it was agreed that the kingdom should be divided between them. Eadmund receiving Wessex and Cnut Mercia. Just over a month later Eadmund Ironside died in mysterious circumstances on 30 November (St Andrew's Day) and was buried at Glastonbury. Cnut became King of the whole country.

Four years later Cnut returned to Ashingdon and as a thanks giving for his victory 'had built there a minster of stone and lime for the souls of men who were killed there; and he gave it to his own priest, whose name was Stigand.'

The statue of Brytnoth at Maldon

Chapter 7
After the Norman conquest

Cnut was succeeded in 1035 by his son, Harold I, and when he died five years later, Cnut's second son, Hardicanute, became king. He died in 1042 and Edward the Confessor was crowned king. He was English on his father's side and the son of Emma, daughter of Richard, Duke of Normandy, who was the second wife of Ethelred II, the Unready, who was also father of Edmund Ironside through his first wife, Elfgifb.

Edward spent 25 years in exile in Normandy, returning to England the year before Hardicanute died. Three years after he was crowned, Edward married Edith, daughter of Earl Godwine and sister to Harold, the Earl of the East Angles. She bore him no children.

Cnut and his sons had maintained a strong standing navy, but all that changed under the weak rule of Edward the Confessor when once again pirates began raiding the coast. In both 1046 and 1049 Essex suffered badly. In the latter attack on Eadwulfsness (Walton-on-the-Naze), as the king's forces were unable to effect a victory, it was left to the North Sea to destroy most of the invaders as they withdrew.

Around 1051, through a disagreement with Edward, Godwine and all his sons were outlawed with Harold fleeing to Ireland and Godwine going to Flanders. That same year William of Normandy, according to the Anglo-Saxon Chronicle visited the English court, and it is thought, Edward promised him the crown of England on his death. Next year Godwine and his sons returned to England and, when Godwine died in 1053, Harold's power gradually increased until he virtually ruled England during the last thirteen years of Edward's reign. On Edward's death on 6 January, 1066, Harold was elected King at a meeting in London by the lords of Wessex.

Before the two contestants met outside Hastings on 14 October, Harold was to spend some time as a guest, albeit a reluctant one, of William, Duke of Normandy, in France. As is well known, Harold II, King of England, and former Earl of Essex, was killed during the battle, leaving William the victor. Many historians see the victory as a triumph of eleventh century military techniques over seventh century methods: Harold relied on the shield wall, with no cavalry and very few archers, while William had bowmen and shoed and strirruped horses.

Although a large number of the English nobility died in the battle, William was still concerned that the power of those remaining should not be turned against him. He therefore arranged that the country was divided up among his supporters. Their holdings and manors were spread throughout the country in small parcels. Even here William was determined that his loyal knights would not be able to become powerful enough, either singly, or by banding together, to rise against him. Their support was essential, however, for the defence of the realm whether from the Saxons internally, or invaders from across the water.

Being a foreigner, the King was not very popular with the native English, so for security William began building castles, of which the Tower of London, Windsor and Colchester are examples, in every major town that he conquered. By 1100 it is said that there were at least 500 Norman castles spread at strategic locations throughout the English countryside. In most cases these would not be the stone fortresses we see today, but wooden structures such as they built in Normandy, known as a motto and bailey.

These were not the first castles to be built in England. An early version called a ringwork consisted of a ditch and bank with a palisade at the top enclosing the accommodation. An example of this type of castle can be found in the north-west corner of the county at Chrishall.

From about 1050 the Normans had been using a system of 'instant' castles they had developed. Local labour would be used and the whole structure could be erected very rapidly. It consisted of a mound of earth (*motte*), generally about 50 ft (15 m) high, resulting from the digging of a circular ditch. On top the mound was ringed by a wooden stockade enclosing a tower or keep (*donjon*) consisting of two - sometimes three - storeys, designed not only for defence, but for housing store rooms, soldiers' quarters and living accommodation for the lord and his family.

At ground level encircling the motte and its ditch would be another stockade and ditch forming the outer defensive area known as the bailey. If there was sufficient suitable land outside the bailey sometimes a second, or outer, bailey would be erected for extra security.

Outside the palisade all undergrowth and trees would be removed to give an uninterrupted view and open ground to prevent surprise attacks. The primary role of any castle is to prevent freedom of movement to the enemy. The first motte and bailey on English soil was built at Pevensey by William to protect his beachhead soon after he landed, and its erection is shown in the Bayeux Tapestry.

Fire, siege and the passage of time could destroy the buildings on top of the motte but once created the foundation site was not so easily razed, which is why so many former castles have been recognised by their grassy humps. Pleshey is a classic example in Essex where the motte dominates both the village and the surrounding countryside.

Fire used by an attacking force was always the worst fear of the defenders in a wooden castle. If the wooden parts were burnt down the earthworks still remained and another donjon could be built on top. The next logical step was to build a masonry keep with thick walls and small windows, and replace the outer wooden palisade with a stone curtain wall to which could be added bastions - a mass of masonry, brick, or stonefaced earthwork projecting from the fortification in the form of an irregular pentagon - to enable defenders to direct a crossfire on to the attackers from whichever direction they approached. Then came crenellated embattlements where the defenders could hurl missiles at their attackers. The next development was to improve the crude ditch with a moat which could be filled with water, or left dry if there was no ready supply of water. A drawbridge, raised from within the castle, enabled the moat to be crossed. More protection at the castle entrance, and within the castle, was provided by a strong heavy grating, called a portcullis, raised and lowered in vertical grooves at the side of the gateway. Often as additional defensive measure a tower, known as a barbican, was built over the gateway. Gradually square keeps were replaced by circular towers with no awkward corners, which were easier to defend. Most of these major castle developments were taking place during the twelfth and thirteenth centuries. This was the result of the return of the Crusaders from Palestine bringing fresh defensive ideas following their experiences in siege warfare.

Birch

At the time of the Domesday survey the site of Birch castle, together with Stansted and other Essex lands was in the possession of Robert de Gernon, or Gurno, Duke of Boulogne, a knight who probably came over with William for the invasion. As there is no firm evidence that a stone structure existed, it would appear that it was a typical motte and bailey, a wooden tower surrounded by wooden palisades. As Tacitus writes about a 'castellum', it is quite possible that the Normans may have used earthworks on the site dating from Roman times

Chipping Ongar

It has been suggested that a Roman structure existed on the site as Roman brick has been found and material from this period is incorporated in the local church. The castle site is located on a projection between the River Roding and the Crispey Brook off to the west side of today's High Street. The 50 ft (15.25 m) high motte, which could have been erected as early as the ninth century, is 230 ft (70 m) in diameter at the base and 70 ft (21.33 m) at the top. Evidence of the flint and brick keep, built by either Eustace, Earl of Boulogne, or Richard de Lacy, can still be seen at the summit.

The description in *Resist the Invader* says, 'This is surrounded by a moat and is protected by a strong inner rampart and a moat. The inner bailey probably would have been used for the housing of soldiers and their horses. This moat is joined to the moat round the motte and is about 26 ft (7.9 m) deep from the top of the rampart. This rampart was probably topped by a wooden palisade, except at one entrance from the town enclosure at its centre where brick rubble, containing some Roman bricks, indicates a possible gateway. The outer enclosure to the north and east was less strongly defended. The town enclosure defences to the north-east consisted of a rampart and outer ditch, the latter being 55 ft (16.8 m) wide and 17 ft (5 m) deep. This rampart probably continued down to the Crispey Brook as did the south rampart which followed the path of the present

Castle Street. The entrances were probably where the High Street passed through this enclosure.'

On inheriting the manor in the sixteenth century Jeames Morrys demolished the keep and in its place built a house, which in turn was pulled down nearly 200 years later.

Clavering

When Edward the Confessor returned to this country from exile in 1042 Robert Fitzwimarc, a Norman, came with him and manors in Essex, which included Canfield, Clavering and Hadleigh, were granted to him. At the time of the Domesday Book these were in the hands of his son, Suene. Following a dispute in 1052 the Anglo-Saxon Chronicle tells us that 'When Archbishop Robert [of Jumièges] and the Frenchmen found that out, they took their horses and went some west to Osbern Pentecost's castle, some north to Robert's castle'. Experts have identified Robert's castle as being in Essex and suggest either Canfield or Clavering.

Clavering was certainly known to be the headquarters of the Fitzwimarc family, so many experts consider this to be the earliest Essex castle - a raised rectangular fortress area with impressive earthworks extending for over an acre. On the north side the water filled moat is over 390 ft (118 m) long and possibly 18 ft (5.4 m) deep, surrounded by overgrown scrub and trees. On the south side the steep ditch has mature trees and the whole site is generally overgrown. Some eighteenth century accounts record some walls still standing, but nothing remains to be seen above ground today.

Colchester

Colchester Castle stands on the foundations of the Roman temple dedicated to the Emperor Claudius and is claimed to have the largest Norman keep ever built, not only in England but also in Europe. Although it is not mentioned in the Domesday Book, the castle was granted to Eudo, a steward (dapifer) both to William I and his two sons, William II and Henry I. Initially, a 13 ft (3.95 m) deep ditch was dug around the ruins of the temple which still provided the ideal defensive site being strategically positioned at the top of a hill. The spoil was deposited over the remains of the Roman walls forming the motte ready to be topped by a wooden palisade. When the masonry keep came to be built the ruins were used as the base. The 17 ft (5 m) thick foundations extend 25 ft (7.6 m).

The keep originally had a height of 90 ft (27 m) divided into at least three storeys of which only two now remain. Towers on the corners rose above the keep by another 10 ft (3 m) to 17 ft (5 m), and extend beyond the walls. The 12½ ft (3.8 m) thick walls at floor level are reinforced by flat buttresses. In overall plan the castle is similar to the White Tower in London, with dimensions 151 ft (46.18 m) north to south and 110 ft (33.5 m) in the east to west direction. Materials used in its construction include Roman brick and dressed stone from Roman ruins, dressed stone from Surrey and Northamptonshire, septaria (compacted clay nodules found

The keep at Castle Hedingham is approached from the east by this Tudor Bridge built by John, 13th Earl of Oxford, in 1496. It replaced the original drawbridge and spanned the moat between the inner and outer bailey.

in exposed London Clay), Kentish ragstone, and in the twelfth century white stone was brought over from Caen in Normandy when the entrance was reconstructed. Immediately inside the entrance is the wellhouse and the newel staircase, or Great Stairs, leading to the upper floors. The twelfth century staircase has a diameter of 16 ft (4.8 m), and the ashlar, or square stone facing, is only applied in the entrance passage.

Throughout the Middle Ages the castle was largely in the gift of the King and could be given to any who pleased him. It was therefore a royal fortress, not a baronial residence. During this period it saw a number of dramatic actions. Some historians consider Essex took a more active role in the struggle for the Great Charter than has previously been recognised.

At the time of King John's war with the barons, William de Lanvalei III was Constable of the Castle - the third member of the family to be appointed. During his reign John stayed at the castle four times. Shortly after his fifth, William, whose sympathies were with the barons, rode off to join them at Bury St Edmunds, where proceedings were started that led to the signing of Magna Carta. Stephen Harengoot, probably one of the large force of foreign mercenaries brought over by John, was appointed to the castle and lost no time in increasing the defences. He acquired eight balistas (catapults), six 12 in. and two 24 in., and fortified the town. Early in 1215 trained engineers were sent from London. On 15 June the Magna Carta was sealed at Runnymede and the castle was returned to William de Lanvalei.

John, refusing to recognise the charter, did not give up his fight with the barons, with the result that later that year 7,000 men were sent by Philip, Dauphin of France to support the barons, and they landed on the Orwell. Some were stationed in Colchester Castle. At the same time, forces of John, under Savary de Mauléon, the Bloody, and the earl of Salisbury, were plundering and destroying the countryside of Essex, Suffolk and Ely.

John in the meanwhile was besieging Rochester. At the end of January 1216, Savary de Mauléon laid siege to Colchester Castle. He withdrew to Bury St Edmunds on 3 February when a baronial army approached, but returned to the attack when it no longer threatened.

John joined him and bitter fighting ensued. The French surrendered, and 150 soldiers, including 17 ballistarii - operators of the military engine for hurling heavy stones - were freed only to be arrested later in London; the English captives were held to ransom. The king then went on to capture Robert de Vere's castle at Hedingham.

William de Lanvalei was deprived of Colchester Castle and Harengoot again took over command. Before this period ended the county suffered terribly from the king's soldiers marching through Essex burning and destroying everything along their route, even the churches.

Under Prince Louis, who laid claim to the English crown, the French again occupied the castle in 1217, retiring later that year with the signing of the treaty of Lambert. That was the last occupation of the castle by a foreign power, although many prisoners, a large number from overseas, were detained there over the years. Among the more notable were Sir Charles Lucas and Sir George Lisle before being shot in 1648 in the castle bailey for their part in the defence of Colchester during the Civil War.

Following the Civil War, Lord Stanhope, who had custody of the castle and lost everything to the Royalist cause, is thought to have begun pulling it down. After much legal wrangling, in 1683 the castle was sold to John Wheeley for demolition; it proved too much of a burden and he gave up. When Charles Gray acquired the property in 1749 he created a library for his own books and made other alterations. During the Napoleonic Wars the castle was used as an armoury by the Colchester Volunteers. In 1860 the castle opened as a museum, incorporating the Essex Archæological Society collection.

Great Canfield

Great Canfield is another of the properties granted to Aubrey de Vere after the Norman invasion. This, like Clavering, may have been the stronghold mentioned in the Anglo-Saxon Chronicle following the expulsion of the Norman residents with the return of Earl Godwine in 1052, when some went 'north to Robert's castle'. The countryside around the castle site is flat, so a 20 ft (6 m) high mound was built as an island in the middle of a stream and the water was diverted to run either side of the motte and bailey. This created a natural 10 ft (3 m) deep moat. Separating the mound from the bailey to the south is a ditch. Beyond the moat and protecting the bailey are 8 ft (2.4 m) high earthen ramparts. There is no obvious evidence of stone being used for its construction.

Great Easton

Like many other Essex castle sites, that at Great Easton could have been erected on a pre-Roman fortified area. The land at the time of Domesday was held by Matthew of Mortain, whose only other property was a small area in Margaretting. The 26 ft (7.8 m) diameter circular, flat top earthen mound, looking much as it did when it was built, was surrounded by a ditch which has been disfigured by ploughing. There is speculation that the mound was originally higher. Beyond the motte was a large square enclosure, the bailey, also surrounded by a ditch.

Hadleigh

With a commanding view across the River Thames, its importance as a castle site is obvious. Surprisingly, evidence of fortifications earlier than 1230 to 1239 have not been unearthed. At the time of the Domesday survey Hadleigh manor was held by Suene and remained unused until given to Hubert de Burgh by Henry III in 1227. Hubert had a chequered career having repulsed a French invasion in 1216, later quelling a Welsh rising, then having lost the king's favour spending sometime

The remains of the large angle tower at the south east corner of Hadleigh Castle. The tower was three storeys high and although circular on the outside, the inside was hexagonal. Located inside is a fireplace and three privy shafts which discharge through the plinth.

in and out of prison in the Tower, before his innocence was established.

Hubert was granted a licence to build a castle at Hadleigh in 1230 and finished it in 1239 when he had to return four castles to the king. It would appear the king retained Hadleigh, for in the following year the Sheriff of Essex surveyed the castle and found 25 shillings-worth of building repairs. At the next survey 16 years later when there was a change of Constables the castle was found to be in a bad state of repair, with buildings unroofed and walls broken down.

The castle was very unlike a motte and bailey structure. It is thought that for at least 130 years the castle consisted of an octagonal bailey with a buttressed curtain wall, with small angle towers and an eastern entrance. Inside was a hall with a solar. Due to the clay soil at the western end, subsidence caused the entrance to collapse and it was rebuilt in a more easterly position.

In the years between 1360 and 1370, when invasion from France was a distinct possibility, major rebuilding took place costing some £2,287 and details of the work carried out have survived. The building had not only to deter the enemy but also act as a royal residence for Edward III. At the north-eastern and south-eastern corners, two large angle towers were constructed parts of which still remain. Both circular towers were three storeys high, and on the inside the 10 ft (3 m) thick walls were six-sided. Located in the south east tower is a fireplace and three privy shafts discharge through the plinth.

On completion the castle consisted of a 330 ft (99 m) by 210 ft (64 m) courtyard enclosed by a strong wall reinforced by several towers. To the south it was protected by the slope of the hill down to the river and the remaining three sides were defended by ditches.

There were D-shaped towers in the northern and southern walls and small square towers at either end of the western wall with a rectangular bastion in the middle. Due to the changes at the eastern end, a new entrance became necessary and was positioned to the north, where a deep defensive pit was dug, and a swing bridge, barbican, and portcullis built. The principal domestic buildings of great hall, kitchens, pantry, buttery and other offices were at the west end of the courtyard.

More than 100 tons of Reigate stone and Kentish ragstone was ferried across the Thames, chalk was brought from Greenhithe, sea sand from Prittlewell and local estates supplied the timber. Glass was ordered from 'William Glasiere of Reilee' and decorated tiles were brought from Flanders.

In 1377, prior to the Peasants' Revolt, the constable, Walter Whithouse, was authorized to guard the castle 'with sufficient men and archers'. At the time of the rebellion the castle was still strongly guarded, but whether Richard II stayed there during his time in the county after the event is not recorded.

Shortly after it was sold to Lord Richard Rich for £700 around 1552 he began to systematically demolish the building and sell off the materials, some for incorporation into local buildings.

Hedingham Castle's great Norman keep was built by Aubrey de Vere in about 1140, with walls 12 feet thick at the base tapering to 10 ft at the top, 100 ft above the ground. It was successfully besieged by King John in 1216, but in 1217 following a desperate siege, it was retaken by soldiers led by the Dauphin of France.

Castle Hedingham

Castle Hedingham was once said to be one of the strongest castles in England. Today it is privately owned and opened to the public during the summer months. Built in the twelfth century - it is said to have been started about 1130 - the castle was one of the many East Anglian estates held by the earls of Oxford, the de Vere family.

The de Veres feature very prominently in mediæval history, and this particular castle was besieged by King John in 1216. The second Earl, Aubrey, supported John. On his death, Robert, his brother who succeeded him, was opposed to the king, and was one of the 25 barons in favour of John signing Magna Carta. For this action he was excommunicated. The following year, John successfully besieged and took Colchester Castle. Although the French, who were occupying the castle at the time, surrendered, Robert was still keen to place the French Dauphin on the English throne. Aware of this, the king immediately left Colchester and headed for Hedingham to lay siege to the castle. It was taken after great resistance.

In 1217, Louis, Dauphin of France, landed an army at Sandwich and captured Rochester Castle. He proceeded to Hedingham and lay siege to the castle. Again, fierce fighting ensued before the castle was taken. The castle surrendered to the French, together with Colchester, Orford and Norwich. Later in the year, following French defeat on land and at sea, a truce was declared and the invasion force returned to France. On John's death, Robert de Vere, with other barons, made his peace with the new king, Henry III, and returned to Hedingham.

Dominating the Colne Valley the stone faced keep, built on a mound and constructed of flints and stones, is said to be among the best examples of Norman military architecture still standing. It consists of a magnificent three-storey tower, with walls between 11 ft (3.3 m) to 13 ft (3.9 m) thick, and standing nearly 100 ft (30.5 m) high. Inside the spiral staircase winds from left to right so that a defender would have his sword arm clear for fighting. The main, or banqueting, hall was two storeys high, and features one of the largest arches still standing from this period. At one time the keep supported four turrets, but today only two turrets at opposite corners remain to command a wonderful view of the crossing over the river Colne. There were houses on the west side whose footings can still be seen today.

The bailey was surrounded by a wall inset with watch towers and a moat provided additional defence.

Entrance to the castle across the ditch is by a bridge which was added in 1496 to replace the original drawbridge. A descendant of the earls of Oxford still owns the castle.

Mountfitchet

Remains of Mountfitchet, or Stanstead, Castle, are located about 900 ft (270 m) east of the church on a high spur of ground and consist of a ring and bailey. The circular ring occupies about half an acre and has in the centre a small round enclosure, which was possibly the keep.

The ring is enclosed by a rampart, 8 ft (2.4 m) high and 12 ft (3.6 m) wide in places, containing a flint rubble wall. There is also a 10 ft (3 m) deep dry ditch which is 70 ft (21 m) wide from crest to crest. The remains of what is thought to be a tower can be seen protruding from the south side of the outer wall. The ringwork and bailey built by Robert de Gernon, are said to have been replaced later with stone and that King John was responsible for destroying them in 1215 during the Wars of the Barons.

At that time the owner, Richard de Montfitchet, played a prominent rôle against the king. He was one of 24 barons, together with the earl of Oxford, Robert de Vere of Castle Hedingham, John Fitz Roberts of Clavering Castle, and William de Lanvallei of Colchester, who were elected guardians of the Great Charter. He was also the Lord of the Manor of Wyrardisbury in which the island of Runnymede is situated.

Pleshey

After the struggles between King Stephen and his sister Matilda were over and King Henry II was on the throne, permission was granted to William de Mandeville, youngest son of Geoffrey, Earl of Essex, to fortify Pleshey Castle between the period 1150 to 1180. The Earl also held the manor of Saffron Walden. What the castle looked like at this time is not known, but excavation has indicated that at least some of the huge earthworks existed and that buildings were wood with thatched roofs.

It was while in the hands of Geoffrey de Mandeville that forces of John, under Savary de Mauléon, laid siege to the castle on Christmas Eve, 1215, and also laid the surrounding countryside to waste.

Following involved and complex family inheritance eventually, in 1380, Thomas of Woodstock, Duke of Gloucester, was granted possession and occupation of the castle.

Thomas was firmly committed in the struggle for power throughout Richard ll's reign and the castle features prominently in various events. The king visited the castle and after supper on the pretence of a meeting with Londoners who were presenting a petition, said the Duke must accompany him. On the road to Stratford, avoiding Brentwood, the Duke was arrested, taken to Calais and strangled on 24 September 1397. Later, Essex supporters of the Duke of Gloucester seized the Duke of Exeter as he tried to leave Shoeburyness by boat, but the ship was prevented from sailing by the wind being in the wrong direction. They took him to Chelmsford and then on to Pleshey where he was beheaded.

At the time of Gloucester's murder an inventory of the contents of some of the rooms in the castle was made and is now housed in the Public Record Office. Many items were very elaborate and valuable.

Very little archæological work has been carried out at the site. It is thought that the castle entrance was by way of the island in the moat and access to the bailey by means of wooden drawbridges and bridges. The surviving brick bridge, said to be one of the earliest built in Europe, was erected around the late fifteenth century, replacing an earlier wooden one.

The site claims to be the best example of Norman motte and bailey in Essex. Even if there is little to see today, there is a description of the castle buildings in the Duchy of Lancaster Rolls in the Public Record Office. It was the result of a survey made during the time of Elizabeth I in 1558-9.

Rayleigh

Excavations indicate that Rayleigh Castle had been a large motte and bailey earthwork. Its present height is possibly due to Henry de Essex enlarging the motte around 1150 and facing the slope with Kentish ragstone. Dominating the countryside for miles around, the large flat topped motte was enclosed at the top by a palisade, another one ran along a projecting platform at its base and around the sizeable bailey. It would appear that no substantial stone buildings were erected on the site, although various parts, such as projecting ramparts and the bailey, were surfaced with stones or cobbles.

Under Crown control in the possession of Queen Eleanor of Castile, in the late thirteenth century the castle became a centre for breeding horses. By 1349 it must have been in an advanced state of decay, because Richard II granted his Rayleigh tenants permission to quarry the stones 'in the certain old castle that used to be in that town'. Fifteen years later instructions were issued by Queen Philippa for a 40 ft (12 m) by 18 ft (5.4 m) chamber to be removed from the site and re-erected in Rayleigh Park.

Saffron Walden

Walden (it did not acquire the Saffron until the crocus was introduced into the country in the time of Edward III) was among the 40 manors held by Geoffrey de Mandeville. Little is known of its early history, until the reign of Stephen, when Turgis d'Avranches had possession. Later d'Avranches upset King Stephen, was dispossessed, and ownership reverted to the crown.

It is during this period that the stone construction of the castle is thought to have started.

It may have been well under way by the time Henry II restored the manor to Geoffrey de Mandeville in 1144. The original castle is thought to have been a typical motte and bailey layout with the bailey to the west. The walls of the 40 ft (12 m) square flint rubble keep are all that can be seen today - little of the earthworks still exist. The well, essential in any castle especially under siege, is still in existence under the keep, but has been covered in. Roads on three sides of the site, together with the grounds of Castle Hill House, define the boundary of the two acre bailey.

Chapter 8
Peasant's uprising - the Great Revolt of 1381

One of the first mentions of a naval strength in Essex occurs in 1208 when all its ports, together with a number in other counties, were commanded by a writ of 17 March to have all their ships at sea return home no later than eight days after Easter. There is no mention of why they were needed. The next occasion was in December, 1213, when the port bailiffs were told to send to Portsmouth, within a month, all ships able to transport eight or more horses. They were required for a journey to Rochelle. The next year the county was to submit a return of all its ships, whether at sea or not.

One of the first actions of Henry III on his accession in 1216, at the age of nine, was to demand transport for his army to Brittany from where he planned to recover his French territories. For this he wanted ships capable of carrying 16 horses. Around this period there was an appointment made for the position of keeper of the post. In 1217 the occupier of the office for Norfolk, Suffolk and Essex was Nicholas Donewyz, whose main function was military command on both land and sea. He also had judicial authority on all matters relating to the sea and coast. Later the keeper had powers to compel people to take part in the defence of the coast. This was one of the powers granted to Richard de Tany when he was appointed keeper of the Essex coast during the king's pleasure in 1295.

A method of defence the keeper was responsible for was the network of beacons, similar to the early telegraph system, encircling the coast and positioned on hill tops near the coast, and guarded by villagers from neighbouring parishes. Shoebury's beacon was said to have been the most important in Essex at the time. The post of keeper gradually disappeared with the creation of the position of High Admiral in the fourteenth century.

The demands made on the county indicate that it was insignificant as a supply source of ships and men. For example, in 1294, when the eastern maritime towns were required to supply a fleet of 94 ships, Harwich, coupled with Bawdsey, sent 11, while Colchester provided two.

Eastern coastal ports lacked the enthusiasm for meeting the demands made on them, unlike those on the south coast. On 10 November, 1302, a general order was issued from Newcastle to Land's End, whereby Essex and the counties to the north were to supply 50 vessels. Walter Bacun, a king's clerk who was to visit the various ports to select ships, had no trouble in the south making his choice, but the east showed a general lack of willingness. A writ was issued to county sheriffs, including Essex, on 2 March, 1303, ordering them to take security from the owners of ships for appearance at Berwick, as some had ignored the original order to send ships, and others had not met their quota. A month later another clerk was appointed to assist Bacun.

The king's demand for the services of all his subjects for the defence of the realm included taking up merchant ships and was also the basis for the right of impressing seamen. This constant call for ships might appear destructive to commerce, but in fact the opposite was the result. Voyages in those days were fraught with danger, from pirates and privateers, shipwreck and loss of trade. Royal service at least meant payment for the fitting and hire of the ship and wages for the crew - sixpence (2½p) a day for officers, while the men were paid threepence (1¼p).

At this time there was still no permanent naval organisation. Although the king did possess some ships the masters were generally charged for their maintenance. Whenever it became necessary to raise a fleet of merchant vessels, a king's clerk, or sergeant-at-arms, was allotted to a particular coastal district and together with the bailiff of the ports, chose the ships and men, and ensured they set off for the rendezvous. If the ships failed to arrive at the meeting place, or the men deserted, then the clerk or the ship owner were summoned to find security and appear before the king. At this period there was no laid down punishment for this misdemeanour, usually the king ordered them to be imprisoned, although the admiral could order punishment at his discretion. Later, under Richard II, a statute was enacted where-by deserters were fined double their wages and imprisoned for a year.

Harwich, during Edward II's reign, appears to be a port of passage as well as a trading port, as it is included in an order to keepers and bailiffs of major maritime towns to stop any peer, knight, or any other notable person passing over the sea while the Scottish war continued.

Early in the 1320s Queen Isabella became alienated from her husband, Edward II, and went to France to raise troops. With her intentions known, a fleet of ships of 30 tons and upwards were ordered to concentrate in the port of Orwell by 21 September. The fleet was to include vessels from Colchester, Fingringhoe, Harwich, Maldon, Manningtree, Mersea, and St Osyth. In the meantime, during the main fleet's absence, 12 ships were to be dispatched to Harwich and Ipswich to cruise the coast, manned and furnished at the expense of those ports not involved with the main fleet. On 26 September, 1326, when Isabella landed at the mouth of the Orwell, she met no resistance and quickly marched through the county to London. This lack of resistance is rather difficult to understand, especially in the light of all the preparations that had been made to oppose her.

The Hundred Years' War with France began in 1337 and during the 1340s was waged with fierce determination. Desertion was a major problem as pressed men took the first opportunity that arose to escape. In 1343 an inquiry was begun about the ships involved in the 1342 levy that took the king and his army to Brittany. While in Brest they had sailed away leaving the king 'and his army in very great peril'. Ships on the lists the king compiled were to be forfeited and the sailors, both officers and men, were to be fined.

There were two calls for ships in 1342, one concentrated on the port of Orwell in March and the other, later in the year, from Sandwich. There is a list of 357 ships for Sir Walter de Mauny's task force from the Orwell and for the king in October. Harwich sent 10 ships, Colchester five, Brightlingsea four, Maldon three; Mersea, Pitsea and Whitlowness (or Qwytlowness) each sent one. A later document states that for the siege of Calais, Harwich supplied 14 ships and 283 seamen, Colchester five ships and 170 mariners, Brightlingsea five ships and 61 men, while Maldon sent two ships and 32 men. Of the 32 east coast ports, only four supplied more ships and men than Harwich.

Waging this war was very costly and at times a truce became necessary for both sides as the money ran out. Edward III in 1346 when he led his army into Normandy was forced to make a stand at Crécy. He knew the strength that his archers gave him and decided his tactics accordingly, with the result that the French suffered terrible losses and Edward won a resounding victory. In his army at the time were a number of Essex men as the county was called upon to supply 200 archers, and named towns were to provide armed foot soldiers in the following numbers: Braintree four, Chelmsford four, Colchester 20 - although later they were retained by the town for its own defence; Saffron Walden six; and Waltham Holy Cross four. In addition the bailiffs of the towns of Brightlingsea, Colchester, Harwich and Maldon received orders that all ships of 30 tons and upwards were to be sent to Portsmouth.

In England during this period constitutional changes were taking place both in the House of Lords and in the Commons. The latter was trying to maintain its hold on taxation, not always successfully. Eventually, in 1347, Edward III achieved success in the war when Calais surrendered and England experienced an outburst of luxury, during which the king instituted the Order of the Garter.

At this time the Black Death was spreading across Europe from Asia. It was brought by Genoese ships trading with the Crimea. The plague arrived in Dorset in 1348 and affected both rich and poor. Estimates of the number killed by the Black Death range from one third to one half of the total population in less than two years. Whatever the figure, and experts suggest the latter figure for the county, it had a profound influence on the county of Essex.

Experts disagree with the disease's effect on industry and agriculture. Some say that agricultural expansion was stopped abruptly, but certainly some villages and farming land were abandoned as a result. One outcome was that there were no longer sufficient labourers to work the manors, and this shortage of labour resulted in those that survived being able to command higher wages. Many landowners were all too ready to attract workers away from their native villages, allowing some to break their ties of bondage to the lord of the manor.

With workers demanding higher wages and the produce from the soil selling for the same, if not less than it was before the Plague, the employers of labour were keen to keep wages down. We learn that the pay for an unskilled job, such as fence erecting around the lord's land, was 4d (1¾p) a day, sufficient to buy 2½ gallons of ale, six dozen eggs, or two hens. Also it is recorded that peasants primarily dependent on agricultural production had flocks of sheep of the order of 60, 100, or even 160, while other individuals had eight, 12 or 20 cattle.

In 1349 the Ordinance of Labourers was passed by Parliament. This was the first statute to regulate wages and it fixed a maximum figure for different kinds of work. Two years later another bill, the Statute of Labourers, was introduced to reinforce the earlier Ordinance, by attempting to regulate wages to the levels applying before the disease struck. Stiff penalties were threatened for infringement, but the labour shortage meant that this bill was frequently ignored. It is claimed that in Essex, more than other places, the statutes were rigorously enforced. At Chelmsford Assizes it is recorded that 12 men from the Hundred of Chelmsford were presented in 1351. Among them was Alan Banstrat of Great Baddow who 'will not serve unless he takes for his salary as much as two others take'.

In 1355 the war with France resumed after King Edward received sufficient grants from Parliament. Although heavily outnumbered at Poitiers, the Black Prince was forced to fight and achieved a resounding victory every bit as good as, if not better, than Crécy.

One of the squadrons of ships to rendezvous in Orwell Haven to carry the king's army to France in 1370 was being prepared for departure by a king's sergeant named John Hankyn - thought to belong to the Harwich family of that name. The Hankyn name crops up a number of times in the future in connection with ships and shipping.

In 1376 the Black Prince died, to be followed a year later during the summer by Edward III, who was deserted by all, even by his mistress, Alice Perrers. She is reported to have taken the rings from his fingers and any other movable items she could lay her hands on, before retiring to Upminster. The king's death left the son of Edward the Black Prince as king by general assent: Richard II was 10 old.

That same year, 1377, there were French raids on the south coast, and a new Parliament, which had little sympathy with the common people, introduced a poll tax which treated everyone equally, rich as well as poor. A payment of 4d a head was levied on every person, except beggars. So a labourer paid the same amount as a knight. This was the first time a tax had been raised on people not property. A second tax launched in 1379 was graded by rank, so that a duke paid £3000, a farmer £50, and for the poorest it remained at 4d.

As there was difficulty in collecting these sums in 1381 the flat rate was reintroduced and tripled in size.

Social unrest was still around, a hangover from the Black Death. Labourers and ploughmen were still sought after, and were competed for. Of course they wanted to better themselves, or at least keep their standard of living equal to the rapidly rising prices. Others had moved up the class structure. The lords of the manor saw things differently and turned down the demands for increased wages, and also tried to revive the ancient claims to forced and tied labour. In many places unions were formed to protect the labourer's interests.

Society, therefore, consisted of great variety and divisions, with a considerable gap between the lords and those of the lower orders.

Eventually, things came to a head. As in the recent poll tax introduced in 1990, many of the mediæval villagers evaded the tax by making false returns. In Essex the population, which in 1377 was put at 48,000 had by 1381 fallen to 30,000, while in Suffolk it is said that the population fell mysteriously and dramatically from 59,000 to 45,000 and the inspectors found 13,000 evaders.

Led by Sir John Gildesburgh, justice of the peace, six commissioners were appointed in March, 1381, to investigate the tax returns of the previous year. They arrived at Brentwood on 30 May, 1381, to begin their questioning. Among them was John Bampton who, it is said, was viciously attacked by around 5,000 villagers from Corringham, Fobbing and Stanford-le-Hope. Leading the Fobbing villagers was Thomas Baker, their collector, protesting that they had already paid the tax. To prove it he displayed the receipt and charged the commissioners of trying to collect a new tax. Things began to get out of hand. When the commissioners attempted to make an arrest, they were driven out of town by the villagers armed with bows and arrows, and an assortment of other weapons. One description says they were armed with 'sticks and rusty swords, some with a single arrow boasting but one feather'.

Word was quickly spread for assistance and before long around 120 villages were taking part, or affected by the revolt, mainly in the centre and south of the county. This set the trend and soon villages in Kent, Norfolk, Suffolk and Hertfordshire were joining in. Sir Robert Belknap was detailed to lead a commission to deal with the Brentwood rioters, which promptly generated more trouble. He, sensing the seriousness of the situation, decided that the better part of valour was discretion and withdrew.

Rioting occurred all over Essex. Officials like John Sewale, the sheriff, were attacked, and John Ewell, the escheator, killed. Rebels struck at manor houses seizing the landlord's goods and ensuring wherever possible that the manor court rolls bearing evidence of their villeinage were destroyed. At Wethersfield, Wivenhoe and Moze the court rolls were burnt, and at least a further 71 were destroyed in Essex. The manor house of the sheriff at Coggeshall was plundered; the home of Sir Robert Hales, Treasurer of the Exchequer, was burnt; at Waltham Abbey every record was burnt; while at Colchester a number of unfortunate Flemings were murdered. The reason so many court rolls were destroyed is explained by the chronicler, Thomas of Walsingham. He wrote: 'so that all memorial of ancient matters being destroyed, their lords thereafter could claim no right in them'.

The revolt spread like wildfire and there was a general movement towards London. During the march all court-rolls and muniments the rebels could seize were destroyed or burnt. On the evening of 12 June about 60,000 men from Essex, under the leadership of a Londoner, Thomas Farringdon, were camped at Mile End while the Kent rebels, 50,000 strong, were gathered at Blackheath. During their passage through Kent insurgents released the Colchester priest and agitator, John Ball, from the episcopal prison at Maidstone. They were also joined by Wat Tyler, a man described by authority as 'a king of the ruffians and idol of the rustics', who became the revolt's general leader.

Following an unsuccessful meeting with the King at Greenwich, the march on London continued. Arriving at London Bridge around mid-morning, the Kent rebels found sympathizers who allowed them into the city, where they marched to Smithfield to meet the Essex contingent and set up their headquarters.

During the afternoon the protesters marched to the Strand, where they burnt down John of Gaunt's Savoy Palace. Essex men are said to have broken into the archbishop's manor at Lambeth, and destroyed all his rolls and records. On the return journey the Temple was destroyed, as it belonged to the Knights of St John, the 'black crusaders' whose Prior was Sir Robert Hales, the Treasurer of the Exchequer, and the man mainly responsible for collecting the poll tax.

At dawn on Friday, 14 June, the king dispatched a knight to arrange a parley with the crowd camped at Mile End. Richard left at 0700 to face the rebels. After discussion the king said he would meet all of their demands. When the king had left, Farringdon led a group of Essex rebels to the Tower, where they were able to gain entry, and where they are said to have sat on the king's bed. Later, picking out those responsible for the introduction of the poll tax, the insurgents beheaded them on Tower Green. They were the Archbishop of Canterbury and Chancellor of the Exchequer, Simon Sudbury, whose head was displayed on London Bridge; Sir Robert Hales, Treasurer; John Legge, the man who thought up the poll tax; and William Appleton, who was adviser to John of Gaunt.

Evidence suggests that it was the Essex men who were mainly involved with the Mile End meeting with the king. By early afternoon confident that they had won their demands many of the Essex rebels began dispersing back to their homes, leaving some of their fellows in the city where they sacked and burned the Priory of St John at Clerkenwell, and a number of Flemings, the number varies, were dragged from the church and killed. The building is said to have burnt for a week. Meanwhile, Jack Straw, one of the rebel leaders, and his gang set fire to another house belonging to Sir Robert Hales in Highgate.

The following morning the boy king had other ideas. After mass on Saturday he went to Smithfield where he confronted about 30,000 of the remaining rebels. During the exchange William Walworth, Mayor of London, fatally injured Wat Tyler. It was the king's courage and presence of mind that saved him from being killed. Riding towards the, mob he declared himself their leader and agreed to yet more of their demands. Among them was one that stated no man ought to be a serf, or do labour services to a lord of the manor, but pay 4d an acre per year for his land and not have to serve any man against his will.

The now leaderless bands continued on their way home creating more mayhem. It soon became clear, however, that the king's promises were worthless. He ordered the immediate payment of all services due. Leaders of the rebellion still remaining in London were caught, tried and beheaded, among them Essex man, John Starlyng, who claimed he had beheaded the archbishop.

Some time later the king marched with an army of about 40,000 men into Essex. When he reached Chelmsford on 2 July - via Waltham, where he met a deputation of Essex rebels - he revoked the charters he had granted at Mile End. The rebels disappeared into the woods around Billericay and Great Baddow church. On one occasion it was reported that 500 rebels lost their lives and 800 horses were captured. Order was only restored after the peasants tried, unsuccessfully, to stir up the people of Colchester. When this failed the rebels marched towards Sudbury and on the way were dispersed by the king's men.

Following this disaster 500 Essex men came to the king at Havering with 'feet bare and heads uncovered' to beg for mercy. The king granted them a pardon on condition that the leaders were delivered up, which was done. They were tried by a 24 strong jury and many were hanged and drawn - it was considered that decapitation, the sentence first awarded, was not commensurate with the crime and hanging and drawing were substituted instead - in one instance 19 were hanged on one gallows. Of the 270 people exempted from the general pardon only 11 came from Essex.

For a number of years after the revolt the offenses that occurred at that time were still being considered by the manor courts. At Great Bromley, for example, in the records mentioned by R G E Wood in *Essex manorial records and the revolt*, for a court held on 20 March, 1382, the events of 1381 are vividly described. 'All the bond tenants of this manor, against the law and custom of the kingdom of England, and in contempt of the king and his crown, and to the disinheriting and contempt of this lordship, have wrongfully risen with great uproar, with treason against the king and with malice against Lady Anne (de Leyre), lessee of this manor, as also against Lord Thomas de Morlee (to whom the reversion of this manor belongs), and have insulted the Lady Anne in her hall and threatened her.' It continues: 'they had illegally taken all the court rolls, all the extents and all the other records of the manor (both concerning Anne and Lord Thomas).' Punishment of the anarchists was confiscation of all their holdings.

South of Brentwood lies Childerditch and the court roll for 9 April 1382 describes the happenings there between 10 to 16 June. Richard atte Med, who did not attend that day is ordered to appear at the next court to answer the lord for his offence in entering a croft of enclosed land called Stonehel, part of the lord's demesne, seizing it as common without leave at the time of the rumor made in the week next after the Feast of the Holy Trinity last past. It was well into 1383 before the clerk cancelled the order for him to appear with 'void because he is dead'. By this time the chief pledges being unable to produce Richard had been amerced 3d.

Another villager, John Norforde, also had to appear at the next court to answer the lord for his offence in 'entering the lord's manor at the time of the said violent rumor, and causing all the lord's servants to depart from their offices and duties against their wills'. After this a large number of additional offenses against John Norforde were remembered and reported.

The proceedings dragged on for nearly three years before John admitted entering the house and driving off the servants, for which he was fined 4d. He was pardoned for the other offenses, but as some damage had resulted he was ordered to restore the property sufficiently before the next court, under penalty of 40s. (£2.00).

During the first week of July, 1381, East Hanningfield court rolls tell of events in the area. It is recorded that 'John Geffrey, bailiff of East Hanningfield, caused all the men of the vills of East Hanningfield, West Hanningfield and South Hanningfield to go against their wills to the Temple of the Prior of St John of Jerusalem in England... That he summoned certain persons to meet him at the church of Great Baddow to go against the earl of Buckingham and others... That he also went to the Bishop of London's park of Crondon, and caused the men of the vills of East Hanningfield, South Hanningfield, West Hanningfield, Woodham Ferrers and Rettendon to swear that they would ride against the king whenever he (Geffrey) summoned them.'

On 6 August, a month later, the East Hanningfield clerk was recording in the court rolls the death at Chelmsford of John Geffrey and another villager, and the confiscation of their goods and holding by the lady of the manor:

The chief pledges say that John Filloll, miller, who held of the lady one cottage with its appurtenances containing 2 acres of land by service of 2d per year, was indicted for felonious treason against the lord king, and on that account was taken and sentenced to death and received his sentence before the lord king at Chelmsford, and was there drawn and hanged, and thus received his death. And they say that this John Filloll had as chattels 1 acre of land sown with oats (not yet valued), and also one old cow, two piglets and various utensils, to the value of 10 shillings (50p) in all, which remain in the said tenement. Therefore it is ordered to seize into the hand of the lady both that tenement and those chattels, and to retain them to the lady's use as forfeited chattels, etc. And to answer for their product to the lady, etc.

'Also they say that John Geffrey, a bondman by birth of the lady at Badmondisfield, Suffolk, who was the lady's bailiff in that manor, held of the lady in common with Margery his wife one messuage and (empty space) of bondland in common with Margery his wife one messuage and (empty space) of bondland with their appurtenances called Michaels in East Hanningfield, was indicted for felonious treason against the king, and on that account was taken and sentenced to death, namely at Chelmsford before the lord king, and was there drawn and hanged and thus received his death by that sentence. And they say that this John had as chattels in those tenements called Michaels 2 dayworks - 1 acre, as large a strip of land as could be ploughed by a yoke of oxen in a day, but at this period 40 rods long x rods wide, or 4840 sq.yds - of wheat and 1 daywork of oats, not valued. And also he had timber for making a house, to the value of 8 marks [1 mark = 13s. 4d. (67p.)]. And they say further that the said John had nothing of his own here in this manor except what always belonged to the lady and should be restored to her in this manor'.

During the early years of the 1300s, drawn meant that the victim was dragged along the ground behind a horse. Later, possibly because the offender was killed before the hangman was reached, the criminal was tied to a hurdle. It is recorded that at least one dozen traitors were drawn and hanged at Chelmsford during that period. They include Thomas Baker of Fobbing who was executed with three other Fobbing men on 4 July, and Richard Baud of Moulsham on Saturday, 6 July.

John Filloll at the time of his death was not a young man, as he is mentioned in 1359 when he took a piece of land and at that time he was already married. So it is probable that many of the rioters were middle aged. John Benorth and William Swift, who were involved with the destruction of court rolls at Thorrington, both had daughters of marriageable age at the time of the revolt. All in all, Mr Wood reports, it has been possible to find details of 48 Essex men who took part in these events by a close study of the manorial documents. Most of the rioters were peasant farmers, although carpenters and a fell-monger are included in the descriptions.

Alice, the wife of the miller, John Filloll, her son, John, and daughter, Alice, were able to continue holding the tenements on payment of an entry fine of 40 shillings.

In general it appears that tenants were readmitted to their holdings. In some cases, such as Moulsham, part of the parish of Chelmsford, where the manor rolls were burnt, they were required to submit to the lord and pay a new entry fine. At Wethersfield they had first to show that they had taken no part in destroying the records. Unfortunately for one Sible Hedingham tenant it was recalled that he was also subject to ploughing services which had been allowed to lapse.

Repercussions of the revolt rumbled on for many years and the effects were still being felt ten years later, as the records at East Hall, Mersea, indicate. The early records had been destroyed. When the new lord of the manor, Sir Robert de Swynborne, held his first court in 1391 the tenement holders had to produce evidence for the terms on which they held the land.

At the time Richard II was made king, Parliament decided that in future the country as a whole should be involved with building ships and Colchester, Harwich, Maldon and Manningtree were requested to construct a balinger between them. Harwich and Colchester were rewarded for their agreement with confirmation of their charters.

The coat of arms of Harwich, showing a caravelle

Chapter 9
Mediæval invasion threats

Five years after the Hundred Years War began the naval port of Harwich became a major link in the defence of the Essex coast line. Fiercely opposed by the Ipswich residents further up river, Harwich later obtained a royal licence to wall the town which was to be paid for over six years by taking a murage - a tax to pay for the upkeep of city or town walls - on merchandise and livestock. This came about in time for an expected invasion on the Essex coast by French and Spanish vessels in 1380. It is reported that some Spanish ships had been sighted in the Thames.

In 1385, during the reign of Richard II, when the war with France was not going very well and invasion was a possibility, a local commission was appointed to defend the Rochford Hundred coastline. Among those detailed were Sir Aubrey de Vere (Keeper of Hadleigh Castle), the Prior of Prittlewell, William of Paglesham and Sir John Chanceaux. Their brief was to marshal all men-at-arms, armed men and archers living in the area. They were also to arm all able-bodied men according to their estate and collect contributions of armour and cash from all others not fit to fight. At the sighting of the enemy they were to lead their army to the threatened coastal areas. Although the county was ready no attack occurred. Two years later Colchester's John Gernun, together with Hugh, and Alexander Fastolf and others were authorised 'to take sufficient mariners of the better sort' in Essex and surrounding counties to man 10 or 12 ships which were then to cruise among the sand banks. Over the next few years invasion scares abounded, and it was fortunate that a number of causes disorganised the major French threat in August, 1386, as the country and the county were completely unprepared.

During 1402 there was a French raid on the Essex coast which resulted in East Tilbury being granted permission to fortify the town, and a king's ship - the *Katherine of the Tower* - being stationed as a guard ship in the Orwell from May to October. In 1405 the town of Harwich was again granted permission to use tolls raised on goods entering or leaving the port for rebuilding the castle, possibly the one erected at the earlier murage. Henry V at the beginning of his reign wanted a fleet of his own, but it never materialised.

Impressment of ships at this time was found to be expensive to all involved, and unsatisfactory in use. During the fifteenth century it was applied less and less. For his campaign at Agincourt the king needed 1,400 ships and, although a few came from Essex, most were hired from Holland. This seems to have been the pattern during the rest of his reign.

During Henry VI's reign in 1450 when the war with France was renewed the defences at Harwich, built nearly a hundred years earlier, did not stop a French ship attacking the town. The manor rolls record that the town was 'Pillaged and destroyed and our neighbours to the number of nine killed'. It was suggested at the time that the town watch had neglected to do its duty and as a result an inquisition jury was assembled. In due time - six years later - the jury came to the conclusion that 'Adam Palmere showed our French enemies the most secret way of our port of Orewell, safely taking their ship out, to the heavy damage of the said town and against the ordinance and statute of England' For his treachery Adam Palmere was amerced 6s 8d. (34p.).

In the reign of Edward IV, every Englishman was expected to have a 'bow in his house of his own length, either of yew, wych, hazel, ash, or auburn' - the long bow had been introduced in the reign of Edward I at the Battle of Falkirk during 1298. The best arrows were made of the asp. It was ordered that every man, except those who were incapacitated from age, infirmity or office, were to shoot in the butts each Sunday and holy day, under a penalty of a halfpenny.

Henry VII endeavoured to break the baron's custom of livery and maintenance which had superimposed itself on the old national system 'and to render the county levies free from all baronial influence and loyal to himself'. The military system inaugurated by Alfred, was revived, and re-established by two Assizes of Arm enacted in 1181 and 1285, and other statutes less important. Every male from 15 to 60 was, under these laws, to muster and train to arms under the county sheriff. Each hundred was to appoint constables to oversee the equipment of the men was sufficient. This force formed the *posse comitatus* which when summoned for the military defence of their own county, was bound to assemble. They could not legally be marched out of their county except in instances of internal turmoil or foreign invasion. For example, when England needed a total of 20,000 archers for its defence, Essex was ordered to raise 368.

According to Philip Benton a good bow and well-tried arrows were considered a family inheritance. The butts consisted of turf, supported by pieces of timber and rails. The responsibility for providing and maintaining the butts was the constable's. Again Benton in his history of the Rochford Hundred and the village of Canewdon gives an indication of the importance attached to archery: 'a field to the north of Canewdon church is known as Butts Hill and possibly obtained its name from its connection with bows and arrows at about this period'. He tells us that it was the area where the youth of the village were supposed to practise archery, and where, in the early 1800s, with the threatened invasion from France the volunteers assembled under Captain Barrington.

Further acts were passed until Elizabeth I, when every bowyer was to have in his house 50 bows made of elm, witch, hazel or ash. It was said 'that almost no village was so poor that it hath not sufficient furniture in a readiness to set forth three or four soldiers. The said armour and munitions... is always ready to be had and worn within an hours warning'.

Impressment and general arrest could be said to have come to an end in Henry VIII's reign. His main aim was to establish a great State navy. Shipbuilding practises and better armaments were differentiating the armed merchantman from the man-of-war. Occasionally port towns would be called up on to provide ships, but the costs would be spread across the county. If merchant ships were required they would be hired. No dockyard was developed in Essex, although men-of-war were using the ports. There are a number of receipts for Harwich, signed by John Woodlas, who was a pilot taking vessels in and out of the Orwell Haven, and among them are his fees for handling the *Mary Rose*. Impressment of men still continued. In the war with France of 1512-13, which was principally fought at sea by men-of-war, men from Brightlingsea, Colchester, Clacton, Halstead, Harwich and Manningtree filled vacancies in the crews on board the ships. Craftsmen, such as shipwrights and caulkers, from Brightlingsea and Harwich were directed to the recently built dockyard at Woolwich, to build the *Henry Grâce de Dieu*.

It is only with Elizabeth's reign that further developments in the right of impressment of men came into being, with ports and counties having to meet the costs when fully armed ships were demanded - the principle on which ship-money is based.

Early in 1539 the Lord Chancellor and the earls of Oxford, Essex and Suffolk were nominated to 'search and defend' the Thames and Essex, and 'sad and expert men' (Sir Christopher Morys, Sir Thomas Spert and ? Needham) were dispatched to inspect areas suitable for strengthening. In their report of 16 March Oxford and Essex stated that the inhabitants of Harwich were very keen to assist; they only awaited ordnance as they had built two bulwarks and dug two trenches. The cannon arrived in April. Blockhouses were suggested for West Tilbury (Tilbury Fort) and Tilbury Ness (Coalhouse Point) and by 1540 were built and armed - West Tilbury with 15 guns. The first commandants were Captains Boyfield and Francis. Other forts built were St Osyth - first mentioned in 1543 - and Mersea referred to in 1547.

Around 1545 to gauge the risk of an enemy landing the Duke of Norfolk was ordered to carry out an inspection of the Essex shore to Shoeburyness. He decided that as the countryside had very strong ditches and hedges there was very little danger, and he went on to say, 'I think the most hurt they can do is to burn a town of mine called Prittlewell and another small town called Lee'.

In every county in 1551 returns were demanded of all fortifications, those considered unnecessary were to be dismantled. In Essex Sir Thomas Darcy was to conduct the survey. At that time there were seven bulwarks maintained in the county.

The annual charge for the Essex forts - Mersea, St Osyth, The Middle House or Bulwark, the Bulwark on the Hill and the Blockhouse Tower, Harwich, and the Landguard Point and Landguard Road block-houses - for that year totalled £784 15s., with those at Harwich costing £328 10s. Landguard was included in the Essex assessments.

Eventually the outlay for the fortifications was reduced by £583 12s. 6d. per year. By June 1553 the forts were entirely or partly demolished and the weapons returned to the Tower.

Over the next few years the fortifications were left neglected. During times of peace they had been manned by a captain, a lieutenant and a porter paid by the government. When danger threatened they were supplemented by train-bands - citizen soldiery - from the neighbouring townships, and as the threat increased troops were drafted in as a regular garrison. In 1558 a survey found the guards at the blockhouses of West Tilbury were maintained by the efforts of the surrounding villages. That same year another report stated that it had heard the fort at Tilbury was falling into a ruinous condition.

To reinforce the Calais garrison in 1547, foot-soldiers were levied in Essex, and a number of other men were sent north for service. Later the tension eased as, during 1554, the beacon watch was disbanded.

Around 1557, the Sheriff was replaced as the county officer by the lord lieutenant. He was to be the commander and organiser of the county militia. Frequent reviews of men, munitions and armour were carried out by the lord lieutenant and his subordinates, and as much of the finances as possible were directed towards local and volunteer resources. That the system worked is illustrated by the fact that around 40,000 militiamen, ready and armed, were assembled when the Armada was in the Channel, with more gathering daily.

Ever since John's reign port officials were required to make returns of the men and ships available for service. Many of the early returns have disappeared, but some from the Elizabethan period still exist. One return submitted by Essex for 1560, when the war with France and Scotland was still being fought, lists 565 'mariners and sailors', and two vessels belonging to Brightlingsea - one of 100 ton and the other 140 ton. Four years later the figure had risen to 187 harbours, ports and creeks, 1196 mariners and fishermen, and 349 ships, boats and vessels.

During 1572 a register of coasting traders was completed by Thomas Colshill, a London surveyor of customs, which gave this breakdown for Essex: -

	140 tons	100 tons	50 to 100	20 to 50 tons	20 tons & under
Colchester	1	-	5	17	6
Harwich	-	3	6	3	4
Maldon	-	-	4	6	8
Brightlingsea	-	-	1	10	-
Wivenhoe	-	-	-	-	3
Manningtree	-	-	-	3	-
Bradwell	-	-	-	-	1
Walton	-	-	-	-	1

Hullbridge	-	-	-	-	2
Barling	-	-	-	-	2
Leigh	-	-	27	9	4
Milton Shore	-	-	3	-	5
Rowhedge	-	-	-	-	4
St Osyth	-	-	-	-	1
Canewdon	-	-	-	-	2

Requests for returns gradually fell away, experience showed that as the men-of-war bore the brunt of the fighting, armed merchantmen did little, and only then in secondary operations.

In the year of the Armada help was required from the whole English coastline, which was achieved, not by impressment, but by sending a specified number of vessels for inclusion in the royal fleet. Essex was involved with other neighbouring counties.

In 1583 Essex was said to be able to supply 5,000 men for the army and of that number 3,669 were considered trained. Five years later in April that figure had dropped to 2,000.

Towards the end of Elizabeth's reign archery practise was not so readily enforced. It is claimed that at the time of the Armada alarm not one of London's 6000 trained militiamen carried a bow. They had been replaced by men sporting the caliver or harquebus - early type of portable gun - which had increased in range, its rate of fire and its ability to penetrate armour.

A survey of the coast was made in September 1585 by the deputy lieutenants of Essex and their report said in their view the only weak points were Mersea and Harwich. Another report the same year had recommended that bulwarks should be built at the foot of Beacon Cliff and on the south-east of Harwich. As there was no garrison at the Mersea fort an old woman had made it her home. It was in a bad condition, the ditch had fallen in, the four cannon could not be fired as they were full of dirt and dismounted; the drawbridge was useless.

An order of October, 1587, directed the county to concentrate 950 men at Colchester for the defence of Mersea and Harwich, a further 950 at Maldon, and Chelmsford was to house another 1100 in reserve. In December that same year, Sir John Smith was sent to report on Essex's readiness.

The launching of the Spanish Armada came about for a variety of reasons, including English attacks on Spanish possessions in America, on treasure ships, on Spanish harbours in Europe and English intervention in the Netherlands. The Armada plan as envisaged by Santa Cruz and Don John and presented to King Philip II of Spain was to ferry the army of 30,000 men and 500 cavalry as quickly as possible across the Channel. They believed it could be done in a single night in flat-bottomed boats ceaselessly travelling to and fro landing the troops on either the Kent or Essex coast.

Drake's daring raid on Cadiz in 1587 delayed for a period the Spaniards' final preparations. Most of the Spanish ships were built for Mediterranean use and were therefore unsuited for voyages across the Bay of Biscay and up the Channel. However, Portuguese galleons were available and formed the basis of the fleet assembled off Lisbon. Eventually, in May 1588, 130 craft carrying 2500 guns and more than 30,000 men, of whom at least two-thirds were soldiers were assembled. In addition there were 44 armed merchantmen, 20 galleons and the rest was a number of smaller vessels to act as transports for the expeditionary force under Alexander of Parma to be embarked from the Netherlands and landed in England.

Around this time, Harwich fort was equipped with 46 great guns, and a queen's ship, the *Ark Royal*, was anchored off the fort. The county as a whole was to contribute 4000 men as its share of the fighting force, which was to gather together at West Tilbury. The commander-in-chief, the Earl of Leicester, said: 'They are as forward men and willing to meet the enemy as ever I saw'. Although the records do not state it, it is possible the Essex men sent to Tilbury wore blue uniforms. Earlier records of the period indicate that whenever Essex levies are mentioned, which is not often, they are described as being dressed in blue. For example, sheriff Barrington reports that 200 men sent to Portsmouth in 1563 had coats of blue guarded with yellow. Again in 1585 when Elizabeth sent troops to help the United Provinces, Essex dispatched 150 soldiers - with Colchester supplying six 'shot', and two pikemen, dressed in blue coats.

Meanwhile, preparations for the defence of England were taking place. At the end of March, 1588, an embargo was placed on shipping, mainly to stop them leaving on voyages so that men would be available. On 12 April orders were sent to Sir John Norris and others to make anti-invasion plans with the Lord Lieutenants of the coastal counties. To strengthen the defences they were informed that a pioneer corps was to be formed armed with billhooks, scythes and pitchforks. In mid-June the Privy Council warned the lords lieutenant that the Armada was already in the Bay of Biscay and invasion was a distinct possibility.

Commanding officers were to stay in their counties and ensure that their men could turn out at an hour's notice. To stop any acts of sabotage, provost-marshals were especially appointed to round up vagabonds and other suspicious persons.

Later that month another Privy Council instruction told the lord lieutenants to split their men into two groups. One was a striking force to garrison the sea coast defences to repel the invading army, and the second a special defence force to protect the queen.

In the Thames estuary a bar was laid from Tilbury in Essex to Gravesend in Kent, at a cost of £2,087. It consisted of a chain and a line of boats, reinforced by ship's masts as stakes, which served the dual purpose of acting as a bridge for soldiers to cross from one side to the other, and also to delay enemy ships attempting to reach London. The engineer in charge of this project was Peter Pett and he had the assistance of the Italian, Giambelli. The finishing touches were still being made to the bridge as the Armada sailed passed Torbay. Unfortunately, at its first flood tide the chain barrier across the river broke and took some time to repair.

Defensive ditches were being dug across the southern counties, forts repaired, gun platforms, defensive walls and barriers built. Across the whole land a series of warning beacons were erected on high ground, capable of sending three different messages. At the first sighting of the enemy ships these were to be fired, and the church bells rung as a warning for the men to muster under the lord lieutenants at their rallying points, often the beacons, to meet the enemy. Plans were discussed for cutting and flooding roads, and the adoption of a scorched earth policy. Horsemen, some heavily armed, were set up to move livestock to prevent capture.

The English plan entailed gathering a fleet in the south-west ports to intercept the Spanish at sea, and mustering troops in the south-east to repel any invasion.

The lords lieutenant were told by the Privy Council on 23 July that Essex was the expected landing area, and that the Earl of Leicester was already there. For the defence of the Thames estuary this entailed concentrating 1,049 horse and 10,000 foot at Brentford in Middlesex and Stratford-by-Bow. An additional 6,000 men were assembled at Sandwich in Kent.

Another source states that a further 17,000 soldiers were stationed in July at Harwich, considered a likely landing area, and remained there until the danger was passed.

At Tilbury during July an army of 10,000 was assembled under the command of Lord Leicester. They were joined by at least 4000 Essex foot soldiers. Leicester complained bitterly that as the latter had not brought their own beer and bread he was more 'cook, caterer and huntsman' than captain-general.

Early in August Leicester wrote to the Queen suggesting that she visit her house at Havering where she would be handy for reviewing her army. The Queen was happy to oblige and at the time she wrote her letter the Armada was across the Channel in Calais Roads.

Early on 18 August Queen Elizabeth left St James's Palace to travel by barge on the river.

On her arrival at Tilbury she was greeted by Leicester and 'escorted by 1000 horse and 2000 foot soldiers'. The following day the Queen, wearing a steel breastplate and riding a horse, reviewed her troops at West Tilbury, escorted by four men and two boys. She addressed the men in this stirring fashion.

'My loving people, we have been persuaded by some that are careful of our safety, to take heed how we commit our self to armed multitudes, for fear of treachery; but I assure you, I do not desire to live to distrust my faithful and loving people. Let tyrants fear. I have always so behaved myself, that under God, I have placed my chiefest strength and safeguard in the loyal hearts and good will of my

The Redoubt moat viewed from the drawbridge. Its original depth was 40 feet. During restoration work a 9 inch rifled muzzle loading (RML) Mk 5 gun was unearthed, which is now displayed as the Gilbert Gun. Two more cannon are believed to be buried under the moat.

subjects, and therefore I am come amongst you, as you see, at this time, not for my recreation and disport, but being resolved, in the midst and heat of the battle, to live or die amongst you all; to lay down for my God, for my kingdom, and for my people, my honour and my blood, even in the dust. I know I have the body but of a weak and feeble woman, but I have the heart and stomach of a king, and a king of England, too, and think it foul scorn that Parma or Spain or any prince of Europe should dare to invade the borders of my realm, to which, rather than any dishonour shall grow by me, I myself will take up arms, I myself will be general, Judge and rewarder of every one of your virtues in the field. I know, already for your forwardness, you have deserved rewards and crowns; and we do assure you on the word of a prince, they shall be duly paid to you. In the mean time, my Lieutenant General shall be my stead, than whom never prince commanded more noble or worthy subject, not doubting but that by your obedience to my General, by your concord in the camp and your valour in the field, we shall shortly have a famous victory over those enemies of my God, of my kingdom, and of my people.'

At the time the Queen was delivering her stirring speech to her soldiers, orders had already been issued for the bulk of the men to be released to gather in the harvest. English ships by this time were already making port all along the east coast from Harwich to Margate, having abandoned the chase of the Spanish ships off the dangerous waters of Scotland six days earlier. The sea battle off Gravelines on 29 July had raged for eight hours and at the end of that time the English had completely exhausted their ammunition. As no supply ships had reached them since that time they were also short of food and beer. If it had not been for the shortages it has been claimed that the Spanish loses would have been much worse than three sunk and four or five driven on the banks.

While the English fleet was still making its way south down the east coast, a westerly gale struck it as it passed the Norfolk coast, and the ships scattered to find what shelter they could.

It was this event, as the battle-worn ships arrived haphazardly in ports along the east coast, such as Yarmouth, Harwich and Margate Roads, that rumours arose that the English fleet had suffered heavy losses and been decisively beaten. The rumours said Drake had been captured trying to board the *San Martin*, and reported the loss of 15 English galleons. Another story maintained Drake had been shot in the leg by a cannon ball. Clearly, although these reports were false, the Queen's presence and her speech at Tilbury could only have boosted the army's morale.

Among the ships arriving in Harwich on 18 August were the *White Bear, Victory, Hope, Nonpareil, Foresight, Swiftsure, White Lion, Moon, Disdain* and twenty-six ships from London.

Ships with Essex connections were: from Harwich and Ipswich the *William*, 140 ton, under Captain Barnaby Lowe, the *Katherine*, 125 ton captained by Thomas

Grymble and the *Primrose*, 120 ton under Captain John Cardinal. All three ships served under Lord Henry Seymour off the Flemish coast before joining the main fleet off Calais around 27 July. They may have been in attendance at the battle of Gravelines. A number of ships were fitted out and paid for by the City of London and armed with sakers, minions, falcons (all forms of cannon), and fowlers, together with a variety of calivers and muskets. They included from Leigh: *Salamander*, 100 ton, 60 men, ? Damford, William Goodlad, master; *Rose Lion*, 100 ton, 50 men, Bartholomew Acton, Robert Duke, master; *Jewel*, 110 ton, 60 men ? Rowell, Henry Rawlyn, master; *Prudence*, 120 ton, 60 men, Richard Chester, master; and *Dolphin*, 110 ton, 70 men William Hare, master.

Another merchant ship to serve the whole period under the Lord High Admiral was paid for by the Queen. It was *Edward*, 186 ton, 30 men, including William Pierce, owned by Edward Peek of Maldon. A Leigh ship, *Elizabeth*, carried victuals, its weight is unknown, but it had a 60 man crew under William Bower. Among the merchant ships under the control of Lord Henry Seymour off the Flemish coast and Calais, was *William* of Colchester, 100 ton, 39 men under Thomas Lambert.

The *Primrose*, commanded by John Cardinal, was the Harwich ship in the Ipswich-Harwich contingent. Some confusion exists as to Colchester's contribution to the fleet. The Privy Council, on 1 April, 1588, issued orders that certain ports were to furnish ships, Colchester being called on for one ship to be ready by 25 April. Later, on 11 June the Privy Council wrote to Maldon that Colchester 'hath furnished a shippe in warlyke manner, attending nowe on her Majestie's Navie to their great charge', and the *William* of Colchester duly appears in a list of the 'ships that served against the Spanish fleet and had pay from her Majesty'. However, local evidence does not match the facts. Colchester's leaders met on 6 April to consider the Council's letter, and again on 15 April. They resolved to furnish a ship (the *Margaret and John*) of 80 tons, and 'a handsome pynnace', as desired by the Council, by 25 April. Colchester, however, was not one of the towns asked to supply a pinnace.

By early the next century, musters show that Essex was able to put 5280 able men into the field with 3500 of them well armed, among them were 200 horse, 365 pioneers and 28 demi-lances. Colchester's contribution to this effort were 400, 180, 10, 30 and 0.

In autumn, 1624, 12,000 pressed men were levied for an expedition commanded by Count Ernst of Mansfield for the succour of Breda and the recovery of the Palatinate. For this Essex supplied 750 unfortunates, who were sent to Dover on 24 December to share the miseries of the expedition. Within a few months only 3,000 of the men were capable of carrying arms. They received no food, shelter, or money, and many hundreds died. Few of the Essex men saw their county again.

Also in 1624, war with Spain was renewed, leading to increased activity by the Dunkirkers - privateers from Dunkirk. Although measures were taken to combat the menace, they had no effect. This led to a report in the county in 1628 saying they had landed at Wakering and had set fire to the village while the people fled. The county levies mustered at Chelmsford. What actually happened was that an unknown fishing boat entered Wakering Haven and was mistakenly identified as one of the raiders.

The renewal of war also drew attention to the lack of defences along the Essex coast, and in particular to Harwich which was thought vulnerable to attack from the Low Countries. Sir John Coke, who was investigating the restoration of neglected forts in the home counties, wrote to the Duke of Buckingham in August, 1625, to the effect that 'there is a place which I conceive to be of greater importance, and in most danger to be surprised, namely Harwich, where I understand all the ordnance is dismounted and the platforms decayed and the forts abandoned, so as a few Dunkirkers may without interruption enter that harbour and first burn 50 or 60 of Newcastle ships which are laid up, and then landing a few men may burn that rich town... this place, then above all others, must be considered of'.

The result was the immediate dispatch of 3,000 Essex train-bands to the town, leaving the rest of the county in a panic at being defenceless. This might be overreaction on the part of the Essex population, as the train-bands had no ammunition.

The Ordnance Office books of 1631 list East Mersea, Tilbury, Harwich and Landguard as effective Essex forts. Five years later the annual cost of Tilbury was given as £97, but by the end of the decade the fort was in such a ruinous state that the tide was said 'to flow in and out'. The situation was no different at Harwich which was described as being in an equally ruinous state.

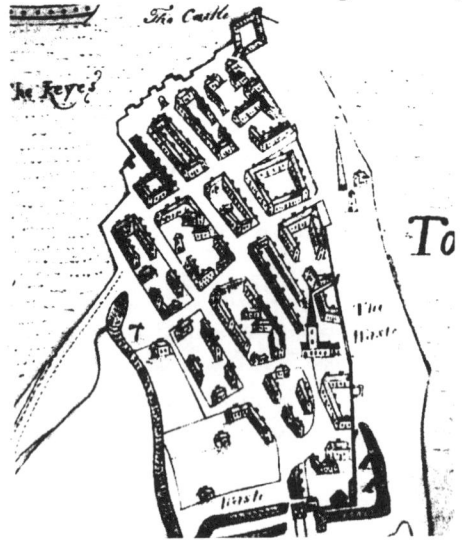

Harwich in 1600

Chapter 10
Civil war - the siege of Colchester

Ship money - a bone of contention during Elizabeth I's reign - continued to remain so during the Stuart period.

From the time of Alfred the Great, the coast of England had been defended from attack by a navy. For many years it had been thought reasonable and fair that the upkeep of this force in times of war or danger, should be paid for by those people living in the counties bordering the sea. This levy was popularly known as 'Ship Money'.

Around the time Charles I came to the throne in 1625 an invasion of the Essex coast from Dunkirk was expected. The likely landing site was Harwich. The expected event resulted in a rehearsal for the later demand for ship money. The Privy Council ordered the county to garrison Harwich and Landguard as part of the defence commitment, and the expenses incurred would be repaid. This the Privy Council failed to do. It also failed to provide fortifications. The Harwich defences were found to be non-existent; the forts abandoned, the ordnance dismounted, and the platforms decayed. The men though were in position during late August.

The Council authorised £300 for fortifications on 31 August, and dispatched an officer to exercise the troops. A few days later it was reported the men were there, but no cannon or fortifications. A report seven days later said 3000 men were in position with no ammunition.

The captains had brought the men to the site at their own expense, and could no longer go on paying for them to serve the king. An order was made for surrounding counties to contribute, but at the same time Essex was urged to levy money which the king would repay.

By mid-September, between £4000 to £5000 had been raised and spent by Essex for the upkeep of its soldiers. The county then gave notice that it would refuse any further payment of such an excessive and unprecedented charge.

The county's applications for repayment of various charges continued for a number of years, as did the arguments over the supply of ships and men and the billeting of soldiers on poor people.

In 1626 Charles I, seeking additional ships for his fleet decided to follow the precedent set by Elizabeth, and summoned the shires around the coast to supply 56 vessels. Due to the outcry and as the situation was not critical, he withdrew his demand. However, on 20 October, 1634, writs were issued to places on the coast. For this exercise Essex ports and villages were coupled with those of Suffolk to supply one 700 ton ship, together with 200 men. The vessel was to be victualled, armed, and complete with stores to last 26 weeks' service. As the boat was bigger than any of the ports in the two counties could handle, they were informed that the equivalent in money would be accepted by the Treasury and the sum they were expected to raise was £6,615, out of a writ total across the whole country of £104,252. Again, there were loud murmurings. A year later on 4 August, 1635, a second writ was issued in which the general total for the country was £208,900, and Essex was told to collect £8,000. Protests now were even louder.

Rochford Hundred, for example, had to raise £308 1s., and the assessment for each parish within the Hundred was:

Parish	Amount £ s d	No. of persons assessed
Prittlewell	28.11.08	68
(including Milton hamlet)		
Canewdon	28.00.00	46
Rochford	11.13.01	73
Barling	11.00.00	38
Rayleigh	26.00.09	83
Paglesham	9.10.00	26
Leigh	25.08.00	85
Little Wakering	8.00.00	34
Foulness	22.19.00	25
Hadleigh	8.00.00	27
Hockley	16.02.08	47
South Fambridge	7.10.00	11
Wakering	15.09.06	51
North Shoebury	6.10.00	17
Rawreth	13.09.10	24
South Shoebury	6.00.0	18
Southchurch	12.10.00	26
Ashingdon	5.19.06	13
Eastwood	12.05.00	51
Hawkwell	5.12.02	25
Great Stambridge	12.00.01	32
Little Stambridge	4.16.06	14

The above assessments give an indication of the relative importance of the parishes at that time. Although the tax was largely based on land, other criteria were included in the calculations so it is not safe to use these values as the only guide to consequence. Also important was the size of the town or village. The list of subscribers in most cases included the Christian name with the surname, but for some unknown reason this detail was missing from the Canewdon schedule and in a third of the entries the term 'goodman', meaning yeoman, was used instead.

For the third writ, in 1636, the county was assessed for a vessel of 800 tons, a crew of 320 men, with suitable armaments and supplies, or settle for a payment of £8,000. Essex found it easier to furnish the ship or the money than it did to find the men. This is shown by the fact that the vice-admiral of the county when summoned to supply 150 press men wrote to say he could only find 15 in both Harwich and Colchester.

During the spring of 1639 an event occurred which shows Essex troops in a very poor light. The county had to supply 1500 men from her trained-bands to serve in Scotland. Among them should be 20 drums and drummers, and 20 sergeants with halberds. This was more than the county could conveniently muster, but it said it would do its best. The soldiers were to sail from Harwich. Some of the men marched to the port behaving atrociously on the way. Besides robbing and upsetting passers-by on the route, they robbed houses, and killed a woman and child. The following year, during May, a further 700 men were ordered to be pressed, together with 60 horses, and sent north to Lord Newcastle for artillery duties.

From the time Charles I succeeded to the throne in 1625, Parliament and the king were continually at loggerheads. The situation came to a head in 1642, with the outbreak of the first Civil War. The differences centred on the king's unconstitutional acts, eventually becoming a struggle over the relative powers of crown and Parliament. The result was a conflict between the king and the Royalists, or Cavaliers, on the one side and the Parliamentarians, or Roundheads, on the other.

Between 1634 and 1636 Charles I attempted to levy the Ship Money tax on the whole of the country in peacetime and without parliamentary consent. This aroused strong resentment from John Hampden, MP, who together with several others refused to pay. In Essex, at Dedham, Samuel Sherman and two other men refused to collect the tax. In 1641 Parliament declared the tax illegal.

During that period there were various indications that Essex people were inclined to the Parliamentarian side. In addition to the refusal to collect Ship Money, there was resentment at Waltham Forest when the king restored the ancient boundaries so that he could levy fines on all holders for encroachments made since 1301. There were Puritan disturbances, such as that at Latton church where the Laudian communion rail was ripped out and burnt by four men.

Laud also reintroduced a law which had been allowed to lapse, where everyone was obliged to go to church or face a fine, which to the Puritan smacked of persecution. Some Essex soldiers declined to march north to fight in the Bishops' Wars, which started when Charles tried to force a prayer book on the Scots.

During the first Civil War (1642 to 46), Essex was virtually untouched by the fighting, although sacking of royalist houses occurred in and around Colchester in 1642. In particular the home of Sir John Lucas was attacked and plundered by a 2000 strong mob who accused him of collecting arms and horses for the king.

Certainly men from the county were Roundheads in the Eastern Association army, as three companies were raised in 1642 and '43. The Association became the New Model Army in 1645, under the command of Sir Thomas Fairfax and Oliver Cromwell.

Leading men in the county were by the sword divided and from the existing records of the next few years it is possible to guess their sympathies. On the Royalist side were Lords Petre and Maynard, the Lucas family (Sir Charles and Sir John), Sir Benjamin Ayloffe and his son William, Sir Thomas Bendish of Steeple Bumstead, Sir Henry Audeley of Berechurch, Sir John Tyrrell of East Horndon, Sir Denner Strutt of Little Warley, John Aylet of Magdalen Laver, the Lynnes of Horkesley, the Maxeys of Bradwell (by Coggeshall), the Nevills of Cressing Temple, the Danbury branch of the Mildmays, the Fanshaws, and some others.

Names of prominent Parliamentarians are obtained from the list of committee men for Parliament, of the high sheriffs, of the members in Cromwell's Parliaments, and those in the commissions of the peace; also the names of the 'Elders' in the Presbyterian division of the county of Essex. For the Puritans the chief of the county gentlemen who served on their local committee were Sir Thomas Barrington of Hatfield Broadoak, Sir Harbottle Grimston of Bradfield, Sir Henry Mildmay of Wanstead, Sir Thomas Honywood of Marks Hall, Sir William Masham of Otes in Laver, Sir Robert Kemp of Spains Hall in Finchingfield, Sir Richard Everard of Langleys, Sir Thomas Cheeke of Pirgo, Sir Martin Lumley of Great Bardfield, Mr Luther of Kelvedon Hatch, Mr Middleton of Stansted Mountfitchet, Mr Henry Mildmay of Graces (in Baddow), Mr Raymond of Belchamp Walter, and several of the widespread Wiseman family.

To these may be added the Harlackendens - Richard and William. Four troops of Colonel Harlackenden's Essex Horse, were at the siege of Colchester under Major Robert Sparrow of Earls Colne, and the Sparrows of Gestingthorp and Sible Hedingham, Deane Tyndale of Great Maplestead, and Colonel Cooke of Pebmarsh - his Essex Foot were at the siege of Colchester with those of Sir Thomas Honywood.

Sir Charles Lucas came from an old Essex based family, and had a distinguished military career. He was knighted in 1639, a few years later became commander-in-chief in Essex and Suffolk and in 1644 was appointed Lieutenant General.

Parliament in 1647, concerned at the powers of the New Model Army, attempted to disband it. At the time Fairfax's regiment was based at Chelmsford, with the remainder of the force stationed along the border with Cambridgeshire. Its headquarters were at Saffron Walden, where long and stormy meetings are said to have been held in the church by Cromwell, Fairfax and their officers with the Parliament Commissioners over disbandment. That same year saw endless negotiations between Scots, the English army, Parliament, king and Levellers, which all came to nothing. This failure to conclude a settlement was among the contributing factors leading to the second Civil War.

In 1648 in various parts of the country many Royalist uprisings, some fairly large others quite small, took place.

For example, on board the fleet stationed in the Downs the Rainborowe mutiny broke out.

The expectation was that the Royalists would use the situation to seize a port and Harwich was the most likely contender. This resulted in Essex's only involvement in a major naval incident during the Civil War. Early in June the crew of the *Greyhound* forced the captain, John Coppin, to sail the ship from Yarmouth to the Downs so they could join the mutineers. When the vessel arrived the captain was able to rid the ship of most of the troublemakers and escape to Harwich. Anchored there were the *Providence, Adventure* and *Tiger*. The crews on two of these boats - *Tiger* and *Providence* - were 'in some distemper', but they were persuaded to return to duty by a Navy Commissioner.

In Kent a more serious rising started, where the Royalists had captured six ships and the castles of Deal, Sandwich and Walmer. By the time Fairfax approached the Medway crossing he was faced by a force of around 10,000 men under George Goring, Earl of Norwich.

About noon on 1 June Goring first saw Fairfax's approaching troops. By 1900 hrs the vanguard was attacking Maidstone and rapidly secured the area. Many of the cavalier soldiers disappeared but about 3000 stayed with Lord Goring, who retreated to London via Rochester.

On crossing the Thames, Goring hoped to gather more support from Bow and Chelmsford, which, unfortunately, did not appear to be forthcoming. His army crossed the river and had some trouble at Tower Hamlets, but eventually reached Stratford, where it billeted for a while.

Meanwhile, the county had told Parliament that it would not pay any more taxes until its earlier grievances had been met. A meeting at Chelmsford of the Essex Committee for Parliament for the purpose of 'appeasing and suppressing the ill-affected humours' was rudely interrupted by Colonel Farr and officers of the trained-bands, who took the members prisoner. That night Parliament received news of the outrage and the following day both Houses passed an Ordinance of Indemnity to every Essex inhabitant on condition that if they would disband and peacefully go home within 12 hours of the ordinance's publication in Chelmsford, and release the imprisoned committee members.

When the Ordinance was published on 6 June, people assembled there seemed prepared to obey it. Lord Goring, who had been joined by Sir Charles Lucas and other officers, convinced the trained-bands to remain in arms as Royalists. Goring's main force, meanwhile reached Brentwood on 8 June and the following day arrived at Chelmsford.

Here it was shortly joined by a company from Hertfordshire under the command of Lord Loughborough, and another force from London which arrived via Epping. That afternoon the leaders gathered outside Chelmsford at New Hall to discuss their future strategy.

A member of the Essex Committee, Sir Thomas Honywood, absent from the meeting when it was captured, rallied the trained-bands he had raised in north Essex and took the county magazine at Braintree. He then went on to assemble at Coggeshall. The initial reaction of the Royalists at Chelmsford was to attack, but on second thoughts they decided to remain where they were for the night.

The following day, Saturday, 10 June, the Royalists left Chelmsford for Braintree, closely pursued by the Roundheads under Colonel Whalley. On the way to Braintree Lord Goring's plan included visiting Leighs, the seat of the Earl of Warwick, and seizing any arms he could find there. Unfortunately, he was forestalled as the steward had been warned of the intended visit and he had hidden as much as possible.

Goring was satisfied with the explanation given that most of the arms had been lost at the battle of Kinton, but Sir Charles Lucas demanded to search the house, especially the area where the weapons were concealed.

A detailed description of the visit was recorded by the steward, who wrote, 'Lucas pointed to one of the places where the said arms were. It seems some traytor among our selves had inform'd him, that wee had reserved some of them. I suspected one of the ordinarie women to be the divulger of it. The housekeeper being by mee, I winkt to him to goe out of the way. And then I called for the housekeeper, with the keyes; seeming greedie to lay all open to their view. But, the housekeeper not being soudainely found, night drew on and part of their armie was marcht away. Collonel Whalley was also at their heeles, and gave them an alarum, so that it hindred any further search'.

He continued, 'So wee lost some horses, two brasse guns, a great part (though not halfe) our armes, four barrells of pouder, some match and bullett; and after the drinking of some twenty hogsheads of beere, one hogshead of sack, and eating up all our meat, and killing at least one hundred deere (in three parkes about the house) wee were rid of our ill guests'.

Colonel Whalley writing to Lord Fairfax, who was still in Kent, urged him to make all haste with his troops to join him at Coggeshall. He suggested crossing the Thames between Gravesend and Tilbury and then on to Billericay. This is the route which Fairfax and his troops take. He then rode on ahead to Coggeshall to meet Whalley and Honywood.

At 2100 hrs on Sunday, 11 June, the Royalists left Braintree to march to Colchester throughout the night. They had a short break at dawn arriving in sight of the town at 1600 hrs on Monday. On the way they were harried by the local populace, as the Puritan vicar of Earl's Colne, Ralph Josselin, recorded in his diary, 'no part of Essex gave them soe much opposicon as wee did.' He describes how 'they plundered us, and me in particular, of all that was portable, except brass, pewter and bedding'. He 'made away to Coggeshall and avoyed their scouts through providence' before seeking refuge with Lady Honywood.

If Lucas thought as a local man there would be support for him, he was disappointed. Instead his advanced guard found scouts along the approach road, and about 60 horse on guard in front of closed gates. Some of the Royalists attacked and drove the defenders back, leaving one townsman shot dead.

Seeing the main army approaching the defenders realised any further opposition was pointless, and on being assured that citizens would not be injured or the town plundered, the gates were opened for Goring's troops to enter.

Fairfax with a force of about 5000 men, including Honywood's 2,000 horse and foot, arrived the following day about noon and immediately invited Goring to surrender, which was refused scornfully. Fairfax attacked at once, hoping to repeat his Medway success.

The Royalist foot troops were positioned across the London road with cavalry on either flank. The initial attack by Colonel John Barkstead's regiment was driven back, but as the superiority of the Puritan horse showed against the Cavalier horse the foot soldiers had to retire towards the town, closely followed by the Roundheads, some of whom passed through the Head Gate. Lord Capell managed to close the gate capturing some of the Roundheads and shutting some of the defenders outside, who likewise were taken prisoner. Still determined, the Parliamentarians brought up a cannon to shoot open the gate, but a spirited resistance from the high wall prevented this happening and inflicted heavy casualties. A contemporary account gave the losses on both sides as 1,500. Two Royalist commanders were killed; Sir William Campion of Lambourne Hall, Canewdon, who had just begun to take an active part in the Civil War, and Colonel Cooke. Taken prisoner were Lieutenant Colonel Rawlins and Sir William Layton. The major loss on the Roundhead side was Colonel Needham killed while attacking the gate.

Setting up camp, and his headquarters, on Lexden Heath, Fairfax settled down to a siege, which was to last until 27 August.

When the Royalists came to take stock the next day they found '70 barrels of powder with some match, and in private houses neare a thousand arms' and at Hythe 'two thousand quarters of rye with a great proportion of salte and wine, which wee brought into the towne'. To ensure no supplies reached the town, Fairfax set a strong guard of cavalry along the Cambridge road and to stop ships reaching the port with supplies or troops sent a party of horse to Mersea to secure the fort. He then began to build a fort, known as Fort Essex, between his Lexden camp and the town.

Around this time the four men-of-war at Harwich, *Greyhound*, previously

Colchester
Castle
in 1903

involved with the Rainsborowe mutiny, *Tiger, Providence* and *Adventure*, were joined by the *Dolphin* and *Recovery* and sent to blockade the port of Colchester. When Fairfax arrived to begin his siege of the town, he discovered two small Royalist ships from the Downs anchored in the Colne. He asked the men-of-war captains to capture the vessels. This they agreed to do on condition that the general would silence the five cannon mounted in the Mersea blockhouse.

On 14 July the blockhouse was captured by dragoons commanded by Sankey. Four days later the two Royalist ships, armed with 11 and 20 guns respectively, were engaged by three of the Parliamentarian vessels. Government papers of the time report 'a very desperate fight' with attack and counterattack on both sides 'with exceeding gallantry and resolution'.

However, it was only when a party of dragoons from the Mersea blockhouse reinforced the sailors that the two Royalist frigates were boarded and captured.

It would appear from the details of the fight, with dragoons being necessary to achieve a victory, that the description in the government paper was an exaggeration. This is borne out by Warwick who wrote on 22 July of the men on the ships from Harwich, that they were 'so ill-tempered that there is as yet no trusting them'.

To hinder work on Fort Essex the Cavaliers mounted a gun on a platform at St Mary-at-the-Walls church, which they named Royal Fort. It is reputed that this gun was the original Humpty-Dumpty of the children's nursery rhyme.

Meanwhile in London, Parliament gave orders for 20 people to be arrested and sent to Colchester in exchange for the Essex Committee still being held prisoner, or to be sued in the same way as the Committee.

Two days later, on 17 June, Fairfax asked for an exchange of prisoners with no result. A raiding party into the Tendring Hundred led by Sir Charles Lucas brought back sheep, cattle and various other provisions, but endeavours to reach Suffolk for supplies was refused by local trained-bands holding Cattawade Bridge. However, two ships landed corn and men from Kent before the remaining cargo was seized by Parliament's ships. Often these raiding parties were the only means of obtaining supplies, which gradually dried up as they met opposition from Fairfax's men, or the owners of the cattle they were stealing.

Strengthening the fortifications continued on both sides, with the Royalists fortifying North-gate and bridge and the East Bridge with large guns transported from ships at Wivenhoe.

An attempt was made by the Essex Committee on 19 June to negotiate between the two forces. Fairfax's reply was to offer exchange for surrender, with the ordinary soldier free to go home, with passes for the officers and gentlemen to go abroad, all arms to be handed over to the Roundheads.

During the night of 21/22 June Royalists forces in the town raided the fort in the Sheepen area, which Colonel Isaac Ewer's regiment was erecting, and claimed partly to have ruined it. This was denied by the Roundheads, who said the attackers were instantly repelled.

By the end of the week guns in Fairfax's new forts began pounding the town, and about 2,500 trained horse and foot from Suffolk joined Fairfax. The weather was reported to be 'extream wet'. Over the next few days, which continued to be wet, various skirmishes took place with both sides making propaganda. This became the pattern over the next few weeks, with occasional reports of the food situation coming out from the town. Gradually the besieged became hemmed in with mills either being captured or destroyed.

Around 5 July the Royalists, commanded by Sir Charles Lucas and Lisle, made a surprise attack with both horse and foot from East Gate on East Bridge, overthrowing two drakes and driving the besiegers into the fields beyond. Having run out of ammunition they were counterattacked by Colonel Whalley's horse and retreated into town, leaving behind the two drakes, 19 dead and 80 prisoners. On the Roundhead side Lieutenant Colonel Shambrooke was killed and 40 men taken prisoner. It was during this engagement that the Siege House received most of its well known scars.

Hythe church was captured on 14 July and the defenders taken prisoner and St Mary's church and tower were smashed by the Parliamentarians with heavy gun fire from 'the biggest pieces of battery, being two demi-cannons and two whole culverines'. That same day an assault was made on Sir John Lucas's house in St John's Green. The defenders were driven back from the inner and outer courtyards into the gate house, where a grenade was thrown in which blew up the magazine forcing the survivors to abandon the building.

By 19 July Royalists were collecting their horses together so that a number from each troop could be slaughtered for eating. Water pipes to the town were cut on 26 July.

By 14 August Fairfax began preparations to storm the town and over the next few days it was reported that the poor of the town began 'to rise for want of bread', and that there was 'a very great floud with great raine'. Work continued for assaulting the town on Friday 18 August, and the next day Lord Goring sent a member of the Essex Committee seeking the terms for a surrender, and a letter asking if the townspeople might leave. Fairfax's terms were that the inhabitants could leave if the Essex Committee went with them. With regard to surrender, his terms were all soldiers and officers under captain's rank could have passes to proceed home, and all the remaining superior officers and lords to surrender to mercy.

On Monday the Cavaliers opened the town gates and told the people to go. Colonel Rainsborowe ordered his men to open fire with only powder, but the townspeople would not stop. So his men were detailed to strip some of the women. It took the stripping of four women before the rest returned to the gates where reentry was refused. After being left in 'no-man's land' for some time the gates were again opened. During the proceedings it is reported that a Parliamentary horse was shot and that Royalists put their lives at risk trying to recover the carcass.

To inform the garrison of the victories in the north over the Scots a kite was flown into the town, and to fool the defenders into thinking an attack was being launched a volley was fired from the Roundhead lines. As the rival forces were so close they tried to hit each other with stones. According to the vicar of Earl's Colne, 'Daily raines, but especially this morning, wee found it exceeding wett.' His diary continues, 'this day a thanksgiving at ye Hith church for ye victory in the north: the enemy in Colchester demanding very high termes on which to surrender the towne'.

Some Royalist officers decided to attempt a break out during the night 25/26 August, but the troops on discovering their intention threatened to kill them. In the meantime Lord Goring and Lord Fairfax were discussing surrender terms. On the Saturday Colonel Samuel Tuke and a member of the Essex Committee, Thomas Barnardiston, were sent to negotiate with Fairfax. His eventual answer was the opportunity was lost for the lower officers and soldiers, and they could only expect fair quarter, all other officers and lords to surrender to mercy, if the Essex Committee were released, a treaty would be allowed.

The following day after the meaning of a number of terms, such as 'fair terms' and 'rendering to mercy' had been queried, the Articles for the surrender were agreed and signed.

The agreement stated that by 1100 hrs on Monday, 28 August, all remaining horses and their equipment should be assembled in St Mary's churchyard, with arms, colours and drums at St James'. All private soldiers and junior officers to muster at Fryers Yard near East-gate, and all other senior officers at the King's Head. Large guns were to be left where they were positioned.

John Rushworth, Lord Fairfax's secretary, accompanied the commander at 1400 hrs when he carried out a tour of inspection. Later describing the scene to William Lenthall, Speaker of the House of Commons, he wrote, 'it was a sad spectacle to see so many fair Houses burnt to Ashes, and so many Inhabitants made so sickly and weake, with living upon Horses and Dogs; many glad to eat the very Draught and Grains for the preservation of life'.

In the Moot Hall a Council of War was summoned to assess the conduct of the Royalists. As peers of the realm the Lords Capell and Goring were excluded from punishment immediately. As far as Colonel Farr, Sir Bernard Gascoigne, Sir George Lisle and Sir Charles Lucas were concerned, the assembly found them guilty. Colonel Ewer was sent to the King's Head to bring the four Cavaliers to face the Council. Only three could be found, Colonel Farr had disappeared, and they were escorted to the Moot Hall where they were told they were to be executed. When they queried the law that said they had to die, they were informed that by order of Parliament all found in arms were to be treated as traitors. They were sentenced to be executed, and taken to the castle.

Sir Charles requested the services of Lord Capell's chaplain which was eventually granted, and they spent the rest of the time in prayer. Sir Bernard Gascoigne, a Florentine, was reprieved as he was a foreigner.

At the appointed time the two Royalists were led out to the north side of the castle, where Colonels Ireton, Whalley and Rainsborowe waited with the firing squad consisting of three files of musketeers. The two men died trading insults with the firing squad and are buried in the north aisle of St Giles' Church. After the Restoration of the monarchy a memorial was erected to their memory, which describes their death as murder.

In all 3,531 individuals surrendered at Colchester. Lords Capell, Goring and Loughborough were detained in Windsor Castle to await trial, while many of the remaining Royalist officers were imprisoned around the country. The ordinary soldier was 'to be conveyed West, as to Bristol, and other Sea Towns, that they may pass to America, Venice, or as they shall be appointed'.

A fine of £14,000 was levied on Colchester to avoid plundering. Fairfax remitted £2,000, and from the remaining £12,000, the Essex and Suffolk volunteers received £2,000, another £2,000 was returned for the relief of the poor, and the remainder dispersed among the triumphant Parliamentary army.

On Wednesday, 30 August, which again was a very wet day, Fairfax reviewed all his troops, including the Essex and Suffolk auxiliaries. It is reported they all shook hands and fired volleys of shot before the Essex and Suffolk men went home.

Various people were recompensed from Royalist sources for their losses during the siege, but perhaps William Woolward demands special mention for his petition to Parliament for his services. He was the commander of a sailing vessel of 150 ton with four pieces of ordnance, which was used to guard the harbour for three months and helped to secure the fort at the entrance to the Colne. In his absence 'the enemy spoiled his house and goods... and condemned himself to death at a council of war'. As is so often the case, we do not know whether he received any payment.

Of the Lords, Lord Loughborough was imprisoned and heavily fined before being allowed to return to his estates. Lord Goring was sentenced to be executed, he appealed to Parliament and was reprieved by one vote. While Lord Capell was imprisoned, firstly at Windsor and then in the Tower where he successfully escaped. He remained hidden in the Temple until the following evening when he was recognised by the waterman as he tried to board a boat to Lambeth. The boatman was rewarded and Arthur, Lord Capell was executed.

Later when the Civil War was over and peace, and the monarchy, was restored in the country, fierce rivalry sprang up over trade and fishing at sea between the English and Dutch, whose naval strength had increased.

Chapter 11
Wars with the Dutch

Under the Commonwealth government the navy flourished as never before, and patrolling the narrow seas was effectively carried out. As more men-of-war became engaged with protection duties against privateers along the entire east coast it became obvious that another station, in addition to Chatham, was needed for vessels to be refitted and victualled. Harwich, by reason of its anchorage and relative position to the United Provinces and privateering ports, was chosen for the task. Its importance rapidly grew such that in January, 1649-50, the Council of State appointed a separate commander-in-chief. Within a short while Colonel Edward Popham, one of the generals commanding-in-chief at sea, suggested that the port be used by two men-of-war for refitting. Later in 1650 a contract was drawn up with the navy victualler for a proportion of stores to be kept there.

As relations with the United Provinces became strained due to trade and fishing rivalry, and the build-up of Dutch naval strength, the English defences were inspected, and the commissioners for Essex were commanded to repair the fortifications at Mersea. Shortly after the war started Harwich and Landguard were defended by 45 cannon. In August, 1653, the Council of State had ordered the demolition of the 'two old forts' at Harwich, and Mersea suffered the same fate two years later. By 1661, it is recorded that Tilbury was the only fort in Essex.

Seamen welcomed the 1652-54 Dutch War as they felt they had some real or fancied scores to settle. In the early days, with few exceptions, there was little difficulty in meeting the demands of the press warrants. As time passed so compulsion became necessary, and it is reported that the Mayor of Harwich had to use soldiers to obtain the men required in May, 1653. A dispatch in August mentions many sick and wounded English sailors in the town, together with 171 Dutch prisoners, resulting from a sea battle fought off the Gabbard - two outlying sandbanks - about 25 miles off Harwich. There was a steady demand for additional men-of-war, and Maldon was involved with constructing the *Jersey*, and Wivenhoe with building the *St Fagans*.

As a second Dutch war became imminent it was decided to appoint a Naval Commissioner in charge of Harwich and employ a master-shipwright. The commissioner was Captain John Taylor, who was sent from Chatham, and the master-shipwright was a local man, Anthony Deane. He was returning to the town from Woolwich having already made his reputation.

Deane was to go on to become the most eminent boat builder of his generation. Within a year his £70 salary was raised to equal that of the Portsmouth master-shipwright of £131 5s. per year. The first man-of-war to be built there was a third-rate, the *Rupert*, launched in February 1665-6, to be followed shortly after by the sixth-rate, the *Fanfan*, built from the smaller timber not suitable for a larger vessel.

Unlike the 1652 war, the second Dutch war was mainly fought in the North Sea, ensuring that Harwich was central to the action. The fleet was assembled, in March, 1665, in the anchorage formed by the Gunfleet Sand, which was to continue to play a prominent rôle for the navy, as an assembly point, for observation, or for refuge, for the rest of the century.

June witnessed the first battle of the war, which was fought far out at sea and parallel with the Essex coast. The English fleet consisting of 150 ships mounting 5000 guns, crewed by 25,000 men, met an equal force of Dutch vessels off Lowestoft. A long and ferocious battle resulted when many of the commanders on both sides were killed. The result was an English victory with the capture of 15 prizes which were safely brought to harbour. A report in October said there were 349 Dutch prisoners in Colchester and none in Harwich. It went on to say that both towns were crowded because of the plague. For the remainder of that year no major naval battles took place near the coast.

The following year France had sided with Holland and an even bigger battle was fought, on 1-4 June. The Dutch ships were now equipped with heavier guns and commanded by Admiral Michiel Adriaan zoon de Ruyter.

Known as the 'Four Days' Battle' it took place off the North Foreland and was certainly a most desperate and unyielding struggle for supremacy. In what should have been against overwhelming odds, the English seamen stubbornly resisted all the Dutch endeavours and fought them to a standstill. De Ruyter in the end was victorious. It is difficult to tell whether the English fleet retreated, but from Monk's fleet at least 17 ships returned to Harwich and nearly all of them were ready for sea again by the end of the month. Now, however, there were very few men left to crew the ships. Unpaid, and half fed they deserted in droves, and the squadron lost nearly 800 men.

At anchor in the Gunfleet on 2 July was a Dutch squadron 'drinking healths, vapouring and firing guns' and at the same time blockading the mouth of the Orwell. Further south the English fleet was assembling at the Nore, and set sail three weeks later, with Prince Rupert in command. He won the battle fought on 25 July. The next day, the Harwich built *Fanfan*, armed with four three-pounders, distinguished herself. Both fleets were becalmed off the Zealand coast. By utilising her sweeps the *Fanfan* bore down on the *Seven Provinces*, de Ruyter's flagship, and opened fire 'and continued this honourable fight so long till she had received two or three shots from him between wind and water, to the great laughter and delight of our fleet, and the indignation and reproach of our enemy'. After the 25 July battle, Silas Taylor, shipyard storekeeper and Harwich historian, wrote that plague in the town was worse, and the place packed with wounded, with many limbless having to sit in the streets for lack of shelter.

During March, 1666-7, the sites chosen for defence at Harwich and Landguard were inspected by the Duke of York. What his comments were, if any, have not survived. Later that year when want of money was keeping the English fleet from sea, Charles decided to seek a peace with France and Holland. When negotiations bogged down, the Dutch to speed things up sailed into the Medway, destroyed the boom protecting the harbour at Chatham, burnt four ships, took the war ship *Royal Charles* from under the cannon of Upnor Castle, and blockaded the Thames.

Those in the Essex militia not already drafted to Harwich, were ordered to Leigh, two foot companies were sent to Burnham, and another two to Bradwell. A company of horse, commanded by Captain Capel, was dispatched to Manningtree.

Around this period an early form of 'Home Guard' appeared. With the daring raids by the Dutch and the rumours of further invasions, it was felt that a land force should be organised.

One method of achieving this would be to arm and 'regiment' the men in several dockyards.

One yard involved was Harwich where Anthony Deane was made captain, and he was to drill the various employees, who numbered 267 civilian workers and 73 seamen.

On the evening of 9 June, Lieutenant Admiral Willem Joseph Van Ghent was in command of the Dutch frigates anchored off Hole Haven to the west of Canvey Island. When the tide turned a party of men landed. The operation is thought to have been one of replenishing supplies rather than one with a military purpose.

Accounts of the time tell of the burning of barns and a house, the destruction of eight other houses, looting and the stealing of several small boats. As this was against the strict orders of de Ruyter the men were subsequently punished for the damage they caused. In addition they stole live cattle to supplement their usual rations. It has been stated in various sources that the church was burned down. It would appear that the rector of Vange suffered during the raid as in his will he asked that 'after other bequests I give the residue of my goods, chattels, plate to be sold and the proceeds to get funds for the repair and rebuilding of my house and barn, lately burned down by the Dutch on Canvey Island'.

Early on 28 June there were said to be 45 Dutch boats within two shots of Tilbury, and there are reports stating Captain John Hesilgrave attempted to prove that statement by firing the two brass cannon mounted in the stronghold. These two cannon appear to be the only two serviceable heavy weapons in the fort. During April the governor had written that the place was untenable, with the walls collapsing and the guns wanting carriages. Five years later, on land obtained from St Paul's deanery, it was decided to build a fort to the design of Sir Bernard de Gomme, and the Water Gate dates from that time.

Meanwhile at Harwich, Vice-Admiral Sir Joseph Jordan was endeavouring to reach the Dutch, anchored in the Gunfleet, with fire-ships. Although a good seaman, events did not go Jordan's way. The winds were unfavourable, and the vessels badly commanded and handled, as many of the crews consisted of the first men that could be collected off the streets of Harwich and Ipswich. As a result of this fiasco, four of the captains faced court-martial, with a Harwich man, William How, sentenced to be shot. The punishment was not carried out. The three other captains were disgraced, and a number of warrant-officers were tried and convicted.

On 2 July, Dutch Admirals Evertz and Van Nès attempted an attack. The plan was for Van Nès to enter the harbour and land troops for an assault on Landguard. Evertz was to cover the attacking force. Fortunately for the English, Van Nès went aground, leading to the raid's failure. Watchers on Beacon Cliff describe how any troops that landed were scattered by the shrapnel effect of shells hitting the shingle, fired by two small boats off Salt Road - now Felixstowe Dock.

One of the Dutch houses on Canvey Island

Chapter 12
Continuing disagreements with France

With the ending of the third Dutch war the hatred and fear was transferred once more to England's traditional enemy, France, and relations between the two countries deteriorated to such an extent that by 1677 war was expected. Due to the work that was carried out in preparation the period became known as 'The Sham War'. One outcome was the passing of the first Naval Defence Act, resulting in a special sum of money being granted by Parliament for the building of 30 men-of-war, with four - the *Restoration, Sandwich, Breda,* and *Albemarle* - to be produced at Harwich by Israel Betts, to Deane's design along the lines of the *Harwich* By this time, due to the increase in shipbuilding, timber was becoming scarce, and while Deane was in the vicinity searching for suitable wood, he visited Harwich, where he marked out a second building slip, and negotiated with the corporation for the enlargement of the yard. At this time Betts was master-shipwright at a salary of £94 15s. per year. Only 18 shipwrights were working at the yard prior to the order for the new ships in May, 1677, by September the number had increased to 80, and two years later, just before the ships were completed, there was a total of 192.

In November, 1688, when William of Orange was expected, it was proposed, yet again, to re-establish Harwich as a shipyard. Nothing much happened until March, 1695-6, when it was decided to set up a smaller yard, and it was then that ship building ceased for a period. There were still no defences for the ships or the town, in fact four years earlier the only defended place in the county was Tilbury, which had 272 guns and only 192 carriages for them.

The following year William, to exercise his influence in military matters, sent a letter to the Lord Lieutenants of counties stating that of late the Militia had been neglected, and that an account of its condition and particularly its arms was to be furnished. In July, 1690, there was concern that the French intended to invade with 'their utmost strength and malice' when the French fleet was reported off Torbay.

An order was issued to the Lord Lieutenant of Essex, Aubrey, Earl of Oxford, to march all the horse and 1,500 Foot Militia to Brentwood, Romford, Barking, Stratford and Bow. It turned out to be a temporary measure as the following month the men were dismissed to their homes to gather in the harvest. The Horse Militia was raised again in 1695 to meet another threat of invasion by the French, and at the same time to meet an additional threat that was being made against the king, as information had been laid that 'divers wicked and traitorous persons have conspired to assassinate and murder His Majesty'.

There is one other document, dated 1704, relating to this period from the Lord Lieutenant of Essex, Francis, Lord Guildford, addressed to the 'Chief Constables of the Hundred of Barstable' ordering the assembly of the troop in that district at The

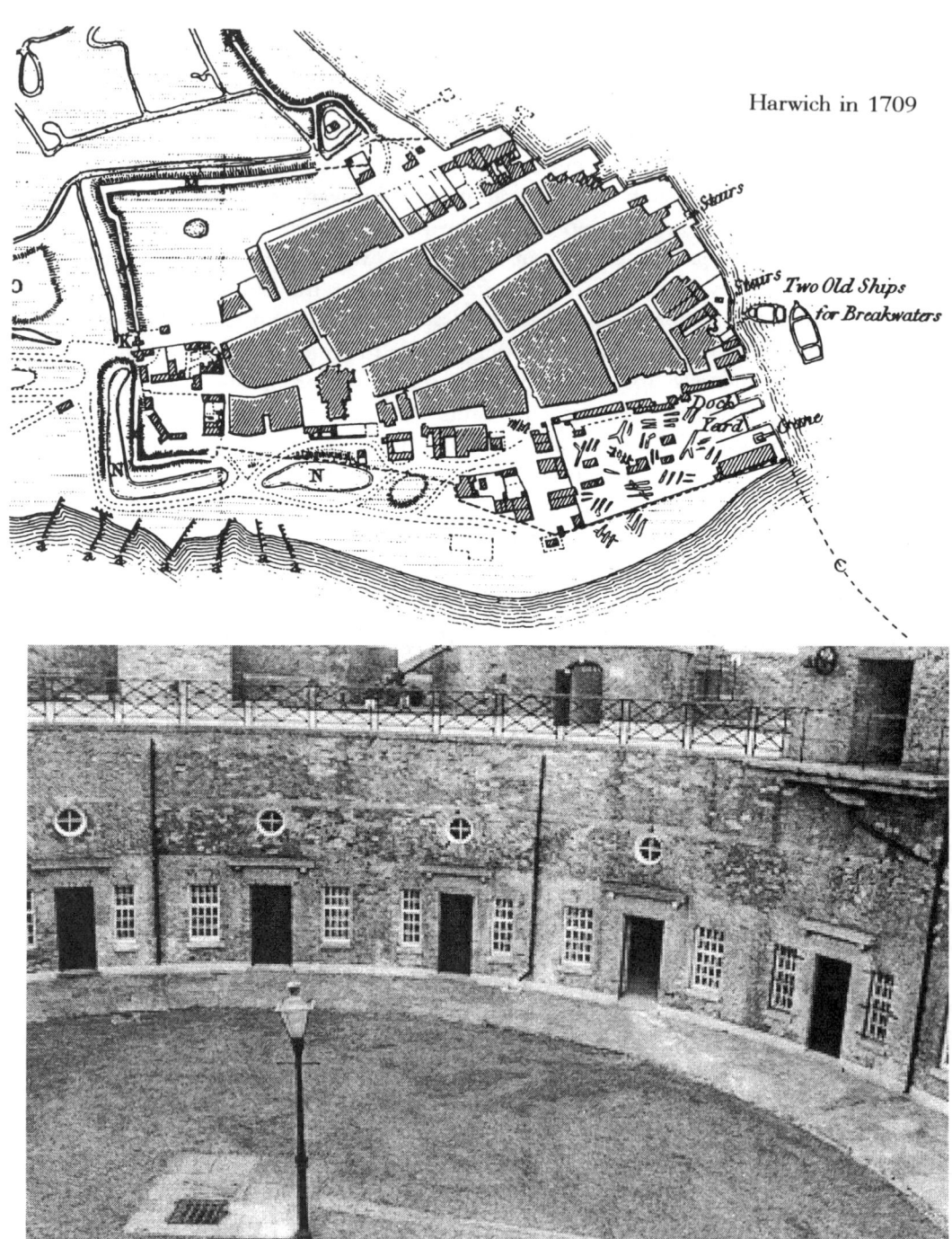

Harwich in 1709

Two Old Ships
for Breakwaters

Harwich Redoubt centre parade, 85 feet in diameter, seen from the upper level. In the foreground the grid protects the well which provided the drinking water. Originally equipped to house six officers and 250 soldiers, under siege conditions about 300 troops could be sustained.

Crown, Epping. The soldiers were to muster at the colours completely armed, with buff coats, buff gauntlet gloves, able and sufficient horses, good carbines, pistols and swords, red cloaks, black hats laced with gold, jack boots and all other accoutrements. In addition, the troops were to be supplied with two days' pay and a half a pound of powder, with bullet in proportion.

The Harwich yard really came to the fore during 1708, when its importance was marked with the appointment of Captain Richard Edwards in the newly appointed post of superintendent, indicating that a considerable number of commissioned ships was using the port. As result attention was once more focused on the fortifications. Still nothing was done, but this could be accounted for by a statement in 1711 that the yard was intended 'for the small wants of small ships', On 19 May, 1713, the Admiralty closed it down, although one naval officer was kept on to attend to the requirements of the cruisers on the station. From now on Harwich would appear to function mainly as a private yard, and there are few mentions of the site again until the middle of the century.

War with Spain, known as the 'War of Jenkins' ear', was declared on 19 October, 1739, and in the following August the Navy Board suggested to the Admiralty that Harwich should be restored to its full establishment. After lengthy deliberations a survey was commissioned to look at the proposal and costings, which appear to come to nothing. It was not until 1742 when John Barnard of Ipswich, who had already built several ships for the government, offered to construct a 50-gun ship at a reduced rate if he could rent the shipyard, as there was nothing suitable in Ipswich for that purpose. Permission was granted on condition that the Admiralty could reoccupy the site if it became necessary.

Declaration of war with France in 1743 brought a proposal from the Naval Board the following year for the immediate restoration of Harwich, on a war footing, 'as of great advantage'. The Admiralty, however, felt there were more advantages in letting it continue in Barnard's hands for him to build contract ships and to repair others. A month later after complaints about the lack of defence for the town an old frigate, the *Winchester*, was sent to serve as a floating battery of 20 guns, and as a hulk for careening and other purposes. Barnard won a contract on 10 June to build the *Lichfield*, a 50-gun ship, at £13 12s. 6d. (£13.62½p) a ton (for the hull only), a further indication that the chance of Harwich being restored as a government yard was very slim.

At Harwich a major event took place affecting one of its own inhabitants, Baker Phillips, son of a well-known townsman and Harwich pilot. He was second lieutenant of the 44 gun ship, the *Anglesea*. Shortly after leaving Kinsale on 29 March, 1745, the *Anglesea* encountered a far stronger French ship, *L'Apollon*, and during the action that followed the ship was very badly handled. Early in the engagement the captain, Jacob Elton, was killed - fortunately as it turned out. The master was also killed, the first lieutenant was missing, leaving command to Phillips who proved to be unequal to the task. Although some of the men still standing to the guns cursed him for his lack of resistance, he surrendered.

A court martial was convened and he was tried on 25 June. A strong opinion was expressed by the court that Elton did not clear his ship for action in time - it was claimed that he mistook *L'Apollon* for his consort, the *Augusta*, and did not trouble to make the private signal, although a neutral trading ship had warned him he was approaching a French man-of-war - 'nor did he afterwards behave like an officer or a seaman, which was the cause of the ship being left to Lieutenant Phillips in such distress and confusion.' The death sentence was passed on Phillips because he did not 'endeavour to remedy the confusion to the utmost of his power, nor properly encourage the men to fight.' The third officer was cashiered, and the boatswain reduced before the mast. The 10 captains comprising the court-martial recommended mercy 'having regard to the distress and confusion the ship was in at Captain Elton's death', but the president, Vice-Admiral James Stewart, overruled them. Lieutenant Phillips was shot at Spithead, on 19 July, on board the *Princess Royal*. He is said to have died with 'courage and fortitude'.

With the start of war in 1776 which, on and off, lasted until the decisive battle at Waterloo in 1815, it might be thought that these years were profitable ones for the private shipbuilders at Harwich. This was not the case, as prices and expenses were high, timber scarce, and therefore dear, and shipwrights hard to find and keep, for the Admiralty supplemented its own yards by impressing men from private firms. As a result Barnard, and his successor, Joseph Graham, who took over in 1781 when workers on the *Irresistible* struck because Barnard could neither pay them or buy materials, both got into difficulties. Graham's first ship was not completed until 1785. Other Essex shipbuilders employed on government contracts at this time were Matthew Warren at Brightlingsea; and Jabez Betts at Mistley.

Many of the ships built in Essex from 1743 onwards were commanded or sailed under distinguished seamen. Among them were the *Alarm* [5th rate, 683 tons, 32 guns - 1758], *Vestal* [5th rate, 659 tons, 32 guns - 1757], *Centurion* [4th rate, 1044 tons, 50 guns - 1774], *Robust* [3rd rate, 1616 tons, 74 guns - 1764], *Arrogant* [3rd rate, 1644 tons, 74 guns - 1761], *Terrible* [3rd rate, 1644 tons, 74 guns - 1762], and *Quebec*, [5th rate, 685 tons, 32 guns - 1760] were built from the plans of Sir Thomas Slade, and the *Arrogant* proved so successful that she became the model from which other vessels were designed in the royal dockyards. At Harwich the *Excellent* [3rd rate, 1615 tons, 74 guns - 1787] was laid down on her lines. The average rate of sailing of the *Arrogant* under all sail was 9½ knots, but the *Excellent* was rather more than half a knot faster, both being exceptionally good sailers, and indeed, the *Excellent* must have been one of the fastest English-built line-of-battle ships in the Navy. The *Syren* [5th rate, 679 tons, 32 guns - 1782], *Terpsichore* [5th rate, 682 tons, 32 guns - 1785], and *Greyhound* [5th rate, 682 tons, 32 guns - 1783] were copied from the lines of a French prize, as also were many of the sloops, either directly or secondarily through an English model.

The *Alarm* has the distinction of having been the first vessel in the Navy to be sheathed with copper. For nearly a century inventors sent the Admiralty or Navy Board, almost every week, specimens of some composition intended to prevent fouling and the destruction wrought by the *teredo navalis* - the worm that bored into wooden ships. The sheathing of the *Alarm* was regarded as only one more futile experiment, although it aroused sufficient interest to attract the Duke of York, Lord Anson, and others to Woolwich to see it in 1761, when she was fitting for the West Indies. The *Alarm* had a long career, but her most celebrated captain was John Jervis, afterwards earl of St Vincent. In March, 1770, she was driven ashore in a gale off Marseilles and badly battered, but with the assistance of the port authorities Jervis got her off. She must have been a fast frigate, for in February 1795, she ran from Martinique to Spithead in 21 days.

The *Seahorse* [6th rate, 519 tons, 24 guns - 1748] achieved fame as both Horatio Nelson and Thomas Troubridge were midshipmen on board her when she sailed for the East Indies in 1773.

In the matter of prize money the *Ethalion* [5th rate, 992 tons, 38 guns - 1797], Captain James Young, and the *Alcmene* [5th rate, 803 tons, 32 guns - 1794], Captain Henry Digby, were, perhaps, the most fortunate of the Harwich built ships. On 16 October, 1799, they took the Spanish *Thetis* with upwards of $1,400,000 on board, and, although the prize money·was divided with the *Alcmene* and two other ships, Young's share was £40,730, and each seaman received £182 4s. Shortly after this the *Ethalion* was wrecked on the Penmarks on 25 December, 1799, with no loss of life.

The results of the last wooden man-of-war launched in Essex, the *Pearl,* were very disappointing. Said to have been built from the designs of the marquis of Anglesea, neither the builder nor the Navy Board were satisfied with her.

Essex at this period became important as the (gun) powder-mill at Waltham Abbey was bought by the government from John Walton and was named the Royal Gunpowder Factory.

The making of gunpowder, an explosive mixture of sulphur, saltpetre and charcoal, was established in Elizabeth's reign, and an early mill was situated in the Lea Valley. The earliest record for the Waltham Abbey site is dated 2 March, 1560-1.

In 1791 the factory was proud of the double-horse mill it had installed. Four years later it is recorded that gun powder regularly travelled from Waltham Abbey to Purfleet for proofing.

Its method of transport varied, sometimes it travelled in ammunition train by land, and at other times by barges on the river.

Large quantities of powder were required for the war with France, and between the years 1809 to 1815 Waltham Abbey produced the following amounts:-

Years	No. of barrels
1809	20,050
1810	20,688
1811	21,252
1812	21,000
1813	25,060
1814	10,161
1815	15,790

Once peace was declared output reduced rapidly. The amount produced in 1816 was only about 4000 barrels; three years later it had fallen to about 1000 barrels, and in the following years it sometimes fell to even less. However, it was not all gloom, as the records show that there were 34 men employed by the mill during the year 1822. This was due to the large quantities of old powder which were 'regenerated' each year during this period.

The Waltham Powder Mills

Chapter 13
The Napoleonic Wars

In 1792 William Pitts' policy for war with France, now in the throes of the Revolution, was to keep out of it. He believed that 'something more concrete than a threat of world revolution had to happen before he would face the issue of war'. That 'something' happened later that year when the French forces following orders, that stated they pursue the Austrians into any country, chased them into the Netherlands, clearly threatening the neutrality of Holland. A week later French warships were bombarding Antwerp, and by 28 November the city was captured. France refused to accept England's note and declared war on 1 February, 1793.

During the American war Essex was never really threatened by invasion, although there were a number of alarms as there was quite a strong pro-American feeling everywhere. One in particular, in 1796, concerned a small expedition concentrated on Dunkirk that the government thought was destined for Essex. It was later found to be planned for a raid on Tyne or Humber.

In addition to the impress system, or press gang, Parliament in 1795 and 1796 sanctioned an experiment, similar to ship-money, whereby each county was to obtain a certain number of men for the Navy. They were to be attracted by a bounty to be raised by charging every parish an assessment as other local rates. In the first year Essex was called upon to supply 244 and the following year 316 men, which compares favourably with its neighbours. Ports in 1795 were also ordered to supply men and an embargo was laid on shipping until they were supplied. Colchester was assessed at 84 seamen, Maldon at 94 and Harwich at 144.

Also in 1795, signal stations for conveying messages across country were established round the coast. This improvement in communications was necessary, especially in Essex where thousands of troops were marching to their garrisons at Chelmsford, Colchester, Harwich, Maldon and Romford, and during the summer months to camps on the commons at Danbury, Galleywood, Lexden and Warley. Essex ports, such as Harwich and Tilbury, were in continual touch with garrison towns as the regular troops were frequently embarking for the continent.

The signal stations in Essex were at Beacon Hill, Harwich, Walton-on-the-Naze, Clacton, Little Holland, St Osyth, East Mersea, St Peter's Chapel, Tillingham, Foulness Island, Wakering, Shoebury and Southend. Within a few years some of the stations had their apparatus replaced by a semaphore telegraph system. A register of 1811 records places affected as Walton-on-the-Naze, Harwich, St Osyth, East Mersea, Little Holland, Tillingham and Wakering. It was claimed that there were more semaphores in Essex and Suffolk than anywhere else round the coast.

Hundreds of men were employed erecting a system of redoubts and a 30 gun battery to the north-west of Galleywood Common. On Rettendon common men were engaged building accommodation for soldiers protecting the upper waters of

These cannon displayed on the Redoubt at Hope Place, are (left) a 1750-80 English 1½ pounder smooth bore civilian pattern cannon with an effective range of 150-200 yards. Being restored on the right is a 1790-1815 English 4 lb smooth bore civilian pattern cannon. Although its maximum range was 1,000 yards, it was only effective at 400 yards.

In appearance this English 12 pounder smooth bore cannon is closest to the ten 24 pounder guns which originally armed the Redoubt in 1810. The wooden mounting is typical of the carriage supporting the second generation of guns. Dated between 1790 and 1820 this cannon was effective at 800-1,000 yards range.

the river Crouch. Rumours existed that barracks were projected for Harwich, Maldon, Tendring, Thorpe and other sites around the Essex coast, true to form nothing seems the materialise. The estuaries of the Colne, Crouch and Blackwater were each protected by a squadron of gun vessels.

Great efforts were made to boost the militia on land at this time. In 1795 it was estimated that for England and Scotland the entire armed forces totalled 16,000 men - although no reliable figures are available. Parliament set about rectifying the situation by the raising of a Supplementary militia to add 64,000 soldiers to the defence forces, and take measures to defend the coasts.

Seven deputy lieutenants attended a meeting at 'Shire House' on 18 November 1796 to discuss the raising of the Supplementary Militia under the new Act, and the instruction was given to the clerk to inform the subdivisions of the Act. Later minutes record that 'The following week the meeting fixed the number of men in each Hundred, Borough and town (25 in all) to be raised to serve in the militia for the following year to make up the quota of 960 men required for Essex. The total number of men liable in the county was 20,082. Thus one man in every 21 became liable for actual militia service'.

Next the meeting considered the Provisional Cavalry Act, which made it compulsory for the owners of 10 horses to be responsible for one fully equipped trooper. Those possessing fewer than 10 were told to find their horse and man jointly. This was a fairly simple operation to carry out for there existed at that time a tax on riding and carriage horses. For the Act to take effect, it was only necessary for the tax surveyors to attend the meeting with their latest tax assessments. Seven JPs joined the talks and after discussion resolved that, 'This meeting being of opinion from the information received by them from gentlemen residing on or near the sea coast, that in case of any emergency the inhabitants of the sea coast of this county would universally and cheerfully concur in every measure for removing and securing their dead and live stock. They are also of opinion that any further immediate measure would not be attended with any material advantage in the county'.

The new patterns for the uniforms for the Supplementary Militia and the Provisional Cavalry were available for the meeting on 9 December. The package from Messrs I N & B Pearce of Lothbury held: one jacket and pantaloons, with a leather cap and green feather for the cavalry, and for the infantry one jacket, waistcoat, breeches, with leather cap and white feather. As there was no standard pattern for the country as a whole at this time it was an important matter for the Lieutenancy to decide. The patterns were approved with the addition of 'black cloth long gaiters for the infantry, and a pair of half boots for the cavalry'. The only problem now was supply.

Urgency began to creep into the meetings as the danger to the country increased. At the meeting of 13 January, 1797, the quota of Essex men for the

Supplementary Militia was upped to 1756, which now made the ratio one man in 14. A decision was also made at this meeting for the number of men to be provided by each subdivision for the Provisional Cavalry.

Around 24 February the Lord Lieutenant received a request from the Duke of Portland, Secretary of the Home Department, for a return of 'live and dead stock' particulars for parishes within 12 miles of the sea. During the course of the next year this was extended to include waggons and carts with suitable 'conductors', and persons to take charge of their removal, people willing to serve under arms together with the number of swords, pistols, firelock, and pitchforks available, other persons willing to serve as pioneers or labourers, persons appointed to act as guides 'being mounted and chosen from among the most intelligent'. and millers and bakers engaging to deliver flour and bread to the order of the Lieutenancy.

These plans were discussed at a meeting at Shire Hall on 8 February, 1798, together with details of the driving inland of the live stock, the routes to be followed so as to allow all major roads to be kept clear for troop movements, and persons to act as conductors.

The returns for 1801 give the directions for driving cattle from the Essex coast 'should the appearance of the enemy render it necessary' as follows:

Tendring Hundred - To be divided into two districts (or divisions) and the stock to be driven to Sudbury in the following manner: First Division will include from Dedham along the Stour to Harwich, from thence along the coast to Frinton, from Frinton it will have for its boundary the road leading to Thorp, Tendring Hundred Heath, Horseley Cross to Little Bromley and to the 56 mile stone (near Ardleigh) and clear to Dedham Heath. The cattle must be driven across the Harwich Road by the several roads between the 56 mile stone and the Stour and the Ipswich Road, from Park Lane to the Dedham Gun, to proceed by Langham through Neyland to Sudbury. The road from Frinton to Thorp is not to be driven upon, but having advanced to Thorp Green the road to Tendring, etc., may be used. The great roads leading from Colchester to Ipswich and Harwich are not to be driven upon except in the several crossings, which must be executed as expeditiously as possible. Second Division will include Frinton to Thorp, Tendring Hundred Heath, Horseley Cross, Little Bromley, the road by Cats Green to Ardleigh, and by the side of Dedham Heath, from Frinton it will extend along the coast to St Osith Point, St Osith's Stone and continue up the Colne River to the Hithe Bridge. The cattle will cross the Harwich Road at Ardleigh and the 53 mile stone to Boxted Heath and proceed by Bures to Sudbury. The roads leading from Colchester through Elmsted Market to Thorp and Frinton and from Weeley Cross to the Clacktons and Great and Little Hollands must not be driven along. When it is necessary to cross these roads, as well as the Ipswich and Harwich roads, they must be cleared as soon as possible. This Division may make a short halt upon Boxted Heath.

Lexden Hundred - Will drive to Halstead and the Hedinghams. The cattle in the

View from a gun position looking towards West Tilbury. The timber bridge with the drawbridge open, leads to the ravelin, the quadrangular island in the inner moat, which played an important part in the defence of the fort, as it acted as a strong point opposite the main entrance at Landport Gate.

part of this Hundred south of the London Road from Colchester, by the Colne, up the Roman River, will cross the road between Mark's Tey and Lexden with all possible haste and proceed by the Wakes Colne to Halstead and the Hedinghams. That part of this Hundred north of London Road which it may be judged necessary to clear will follow the same route, not to make any halt before it reaches Ford Street.

Winstree and Thurstable Hundreds - Will be divided as follows and the stock driven to Halstead and the Hedinghams. First Division, Mersea Island. The stock must be driven by Pelden to Layer Heath across the Roman River and proceed to Lexden, cross the London Road as expeditiously as possible and pursue the route to Halstead, etc., not to halt until the London Road is one mile in the rear. Second Division. The boundaries of this Division will be the Colne River on the East, Mersey Channel and the Creek to Salcote on the North, the road from Salcote by Packwood to Ridgeways and to Podswood on the West and the Roman River to the South. The road from Colchester to Mersey Island over Mamwood Bridge must not be driven upon except when it is necessary to cross it. Mamwood Bridge upon no account to be crossed by the stock. Unless it is perfectly understood that there are not any troops ordered from Colchester to Fingringhoe, the bridge near that place must not be made use of, but all the cattle driven across the river at Bouncer's Bridge, and to the west of it, these proceed by Maypole Green on the right and Heckford Bridge on the left, cross the London Road with all expedition at Mark's Tey, Stanway and Beacon Farm and proceed to Halstead, etc. Not to halt before the London Road is quite clear of stock. Third Division will extend from Podswood by the road from Ridgeways to Salcote and along the Creek to the Blackwater and by the side of that river to Heybridge and Wickhams Mills. The stock of this Division will cross the London Road between Witham and Gore Pitt and proceed by the bye-roads and cross the Coggeshall roads between that place and Braintree and continue to Halstead and the Hedinghams. This Division must be expeditious in crossing the London and Coggeshall roads. It may make a short halt, if necessary, between the two roads.

Dengey Hundred - Will form one district between the Blackwater and the Crouch Rivers. The stock of this district will cross the London Road from Witham to Springfield and be driven to Dunmow and Bishop's Stortford. The principal road from Chelmsford to Malden and from Malden to Ramsey Island, Bradwell and Fambridge Ferry must be kept clear, except in the necessary crossings, which must be done as quickly as possible. Not to halt till it has crossed the London Road.

Rochford Hundred - Between the Crouch (including Wallasea, Foulness and the other Islands) and Hadley Ray. The stock of this Hundred will cross the London Road between Mountnessing Street and Margaretting Street and proceed to Ongar and Bishop's Stortford. The principal roads leading from the Thames to the London Road, particularly the one through Billericay, must not be driven upon except in the necessary crossings, which must be done as quick as possible.

Around March 1797 the county received orders from the Duke of Portland to call out the Provisional Cavalry and the Lieutenancy decided that they should muster at various places and times as follows:

Brentwood Subdivision: Camp ground, Warley Common, 3 April.

Chelmsford Subdivision: Near racecourse, Galleywood Common, 4 April.

Colchester Subdivision: Lexden Heath, 3 April.

Dunmow Subdivision: Little Dunmow, 8 April

Epping Subdivision: Thornwood Common, 5 April.

Hinckford Subdivision: 50 Mile Stone, Castle Hedingham, 8 April.

llford Subdivision: Wanstead Flats, 8 April.

Rochford Subdivision: Hackwell (Hawkwell) Common, 6 April.

Tendring Subdivision: Tendring Heath, 4 April.

Walden and Freshwell Subdivision: Saffron Walden, 7 April.

Witham Subdivision: Tiptree Heath, 7 April.

The force was organised into two corps - Eastern and Western. Lieutenant-Colonel Lewis Majendie commanded the former and Lieutenant-Colonel John Conyers the latter. There is a record of a muster being called in January, 1798, to enable those men who had not obtained certificates of conformity to receive them. Shortly after this the Provisional Cavalry disappeared, to be replaced by the Yeomanry Cavalry which were formed at the request of the Lord Lieutenant in April, 1798.

A Yeomanry and Volunteer Cavalry return to the House of Commons for 1 June, 1798, records a troop of Yeoman Cavalry with a date of establishment April, 1797, which is thought to be that of Mr Conyers of Copt Hall. The next troop of Yeoman Cavalry, recruited in Chelmsford and district in February, 1798, is given as William Tufnell's (Langley). Then follow Mr J A Houblon's in March, and Lord Maynard's in April. The remaining troops are all given as being formed in May, and they are Kelvedon, or East Essex (T T Cock); Stebbing (Michael Pepper); Tendring (John Hanson); Havering (Jackson Barwis); Uttlesford (R Raynsford); Colonel Burgoyne's or Loyal Essex; Haverhill (R P Todd, jun.); Castle Hedingham or Hinckford (L Majendie); Halstead; Walthamstow and Hatfield Peverel (Peter Wright). The minimum establishment was 40, in two instances it was stated to be 50, and in the case of Tendring it was given as 60. In just four months Essex was able to raise 15 troops of cavalry consisting of 640 men.

The uniform in most instances is not known, however, there is on record a field day, in August, 1798, of the Tendring Volunteer Cavalry, when 45 men of all ranks were on parade. They were dressed in scarlet hussar jackets with black facings, and decorated with silver lace, the helmets were described as 'remarkably elegant' with the name Tendring Cavalry on them.

The need for men was even greater in 1798, when Ireland was in revolt, the fleet was still suffering the effects of the mutinies of the previous year, and the French were continuing to overrun Europe. To overcome the problem a new force, the Sea Fencibles, was created by Order of Council on 14 May, with the aim of meeting an invading flotilla with another of the same character, and of manning the coastal defences. The order applied to the whole of the United Kingdom, especially the area facing the continent from Norfolk to Hampshire, and it was composed of boatmen, fishermen and other semi-seafaring dwellers of the shore not subject to impressment. The men, who had to be volunteers, were offered freedom from impressment while they were enrolled as seafaring members, were paid one shilling a day while on service and were under the command of naval officers. Originally, there were two districts in Essex, the first from the Stour to the Blackwater, consisting of one captain, five lieutenants and 65 men, and the second stretched from the Blackwater to the Lower Hope, with one captain, six lieutenants and 187 men. Protection of the upper Thames was provided by the River Fencibles set up in London. In 1798 an additional South Essex regiment was formed, which continued to exist in 1805.

Supplementary militia were raised for East Essex in 1805 and retained until 1815; West Essex in 1804 and retained until 1816; a supplementary unit seems to have been levied in South Essex in 1805.

All matters relating to the embodiment, officering and recruiting of the regular Militia battalions was the responsibility of the Lord Lieutenant of the county, and he was additionally charged with a similar duty in respect of the Local Militia battalions upon their formation in 1809. With Militia men constantly volunteering to join regular regiments he was continually having to fill the vacancies. Each battalion needed a fixed number of privates, so when promotions occurred vacancies arose that had to be filled. When Militia commanding officers notified the lord lieutenant of men who had volunteered into line regiments, or who were promoted, he had to supply details of the parish each man came from and, if he was a substitute, the name of the man whose place he took. By this means the part played by each particular parish in supplying men to the Militia was checked and the number maintained. This information was transmitted to the subdivision clerks, who made dispositions for the taking of a ballot and, if necessary, prepared and revised the lists of men liable to serve and published the orders necessary for the chief constables of the Hundreds to post notices on church doors and other public places.

Typical of the notices pinned to Church doors is the following:

Raising men for the Army and Navy

ESSEX [To the Overfeers of the several Parifh of Canewdon
1797]
In the County of Effex, and to each and every of them.

Notice is hereby given to you, that the Juftices of the Peace, in and for the faid
County, at a GENERAL SESSIONS affembled under and by Virtue of an Act,
instituted "AN ACT for raifing a certain Number of Men in the feveral Counties in
England, for the Service of His Majefty's Army and Navy," by their Order, bearing
Date the Third Day of December inftant, have appointed one Man to be levied and
raifed for the faid feveral Parifh of Canewdon And you are hereby required
immediately after receiving this Notice to call together the principal Inhabitants of
the faid feveral Parifh and Places at a Veftry, to be held within the faid Parifh of
Canewdon to take into Confideration the moft fpeedy and effectual Means of
raifing the faid Man appointed to be raifed for the faid feveral Parifh and Places
in pursuance of the faid Act, of which Meeting you are to give two Days public
Notice in Writing, by affixing the fame on the Church or Chapel Door of your said
respective Parifh or if there is no Church or Chapel in of your faid Parifh or Places
then on the neareft Church or Chapel Door, according to the Form annexed. AND
you are hereby required to take NOTICE, that fuch Man is to be raifed on or
before the Twenty-Fourth Day of December inftant, being Twenty-One Days after
the Date of the faid Order. AND that as foon as you have agreed with any Perfon
to ferve, you are to produce every fuch Perfon before the proper Officer appointed
to regulate the Admiffion of Men into the Navy, for your faid feveral Parifh or
Places, and if he fhall approve of him, you are then to caufe him to be brought
before two or more Juftices of the Peace of this County, to be examined; and in
Cafe the Regulating Officer fhall reject any Perfon raifed by you, and you fhall
think yourfelf aggrieved thereby, you are to give to him immediate Notice of your
Intention to appeal to the Juftices, at the next Petty Seffions to be held in your
Diftrict. AND you are to make a Return of all Matters and Things done by you,
and the Inhabitants aforefaid, or any of you or them, in pursuance of the faid Act,
and according to the Directions herein contained to the Juftices of the Peace, acting
in and for the Division of Rochford in the faid County, at a Petty Seffions to be
holden at the Crown Inn in Rochford in the faid County, on Thursday the
twenty-second Day of December infant. Dated this thirteenth Day of December, in
the Year of our Lord one Thousand feven Hundred and Ninety-fix.
(Signed) James Davis
One of the Chief Conftables of the Hundred
of Rochford in the faid County

Often these actions led to further problems in the villages, especially for the locally appointed officials, as a couple of further examples from Canewdon show.

John Coote, a labourer in the village ended up in debt to the parish when he wanted a substitute in 1782. His note signed with an 'X' was pinned in the Overseer's Minute book. It reads:

'I, John Coote, labourer of the Parish of Canewdon, being drawn for a Militia man do hereby acknowledge myself indebted to the Parish in the sum of five pounds Five shillings advanced by the parish for me towards procuring a substitute/exclusive of the five pounds allowed by act of Parliament/ and which I promise to pay either in the whole or in part when I shall be called upon by the overseers to do-in case I shall be able and have effects /sufficient/ for the above purpose.'

Joseph Quilter was also unlucky in the ballot for men to serve, but he was fortunate to find a substitute to serve for him. The official printed letter with hand written additions from the County to the churchwardens and overseers notifying them of the situation reads:

'WHEREAS Joseph Quilter of the said Parish of Canewdon hath at a Meeting of the Deputy Lieutenants and Justices of the Peace, acting in and for the said Subdivision (Rochford), held the 10th Day of May 1804 been chosen by Lot to serve in the Western Battalion of Militia of the said County, now embodied and in actual Service, and hath provided Robert Dawson of Tollesbury labourer who hath been enrolled as his substitute and is now serving in the said Militia.

And Hath also made Oath that he is not possessed of an Estate in Land, Goods or money, of clear Value of Five Hundred Pounds. We do therefore, hereby order you, the said Churchwardens and Overseers of the said Parish to pay unto the said Joseph Quilter the sum of Seven pounds 10s which we adjudge to be Half the current Price paid for a Volunteer within the said County, out of the Rate made for Volunteers within your said Parish, and if there be no Volunteers provided by you within your said Parish, then that you pay the said Sum of Seven pounds 10s out of a Rate to be made after the Manner of the Poor Rate.

Given under our Hands the 12th Day of April 1805'

It was signed Thomas Hann..., but the rest of the signature was ripped away.

Joseph Quilter received his money on the 18 April as the ever resourceful churchwardens and overseers used the form as the receipt. They wrote out the details and asked Mr Quilter to make his mark in the bottom left hand corner.

Fencible troops - soldiers liable only for home service - and volunteers were raised, in Essex in 1794. Fencible infantry were formed, and were probably disbanded about the date of the Peace of Amiens (March, 1802). At the same time fencible cavalry appears to have been raised, but they do not seem to have lasted as long. As the Loyal Essex Light Dragoons, in 1794, they had an effective muster roll of over 200 of all ranks. In 1797 there were six troops, those of Colonel

Montague Burgoyne, of Marks Hall, who had raised them at his own expense; Lieutenant-Colonel Scudamore; Major Cross; and Captains Sir William André; Thomas Bundy; and Graham.

The ever-present threat of invasion resulted in many surveys of the coast. In 1798 Brigadier-General More reported that the most vulnerable part to Norfolk was the section between the Thames and Harwich. General Dumouriez, reporting in 1803, disagreed with earlier surveys and considered that every beach, even though practicable, was not suitable for a descent, and went on to give his reasons. Rivers he thought more dangerous landing places. In his opinion the Thames, Blackwater, Stour, Wash, Humber, Severn and Dee were the worst.

As an additional defence the construction of the martello tower was proposed in 1798. This followed a recommendation two years earlier by Sir John Jervis (later Lord St Vincent), who described them as 'a powerful though simple fortification', and was adopted in place of a more expensive alternative then under consideration. Up to 1809 these towers which in a few years studded the exposed coastal areas had cost £2,250,000. There were 11 built in Essex in 1808/9 at an estimated cost of £225,000, lettered from A to K, with possibly the Redoubt at Harwich, mounting ten guns, being the largest example. This was built between 1806 and 1809 and as well as the guns was furnished with 18 bombproof casemates.

Around this time Harwich was especially well fortified with, in addition to the Redoubt, the Anglegate battery, mounting five 24-pounders, on Beacon cliff a battery of five 12-pounders, and to the south of the Redoubt another three 24-pounders.

Towers were erected at Walton, Eastness or Lion Point, Jay Wick, Lee Wick, Clacton, and the left bank of Brightlingsea Creek, and they were armed with either three 24-pounders on traversing platforms, or with one 24-pounder and two five and a half inch howitzers. Batteries mounting from three, to six 24-pounder cannon completed the shore defences. These were situated on the north side of the Crouch, opposite the Broomhill river, a second was on the south side of the Blackwater, two miles from Bradwell Wharf, a third at Brightlingsea, a fourth at St Osyth Stone, a fifth at Clacton Wash, a sixth at Holland marsh, a seventh at Frinton and the eighth, and last at Walton.

On the Thames, a modification of the floating boom defence, proposed in 1588, was prepared for use between Gravesend and Tilbury in 1795, and a five-gun battery was sited at Coalhouse Point in 1798, which 'crossed fired' with two others on the south bank.

In 1799 the number of Sea Fencible districts was increased to three, operating from Harwich, Brightlingsea and Southend, under district captains, Eliab Harvey, Thomas Miles and George Harrison. Colchester was to provide 109 men, Harwich 50, Maldon and Brightlingsea 20 each, Clacton 41, Mersea Island 60, Walton 20, Frinton 14, Southend 29, Burnham 21, and Leigh 22.

The Martello Tower 'D' at Jaywick. The round, or elliptical towers were built of brick with the outside presenting a smooth rendered appearance. Accommodation was provided for one officer, a sergeant and 24 soldiers.

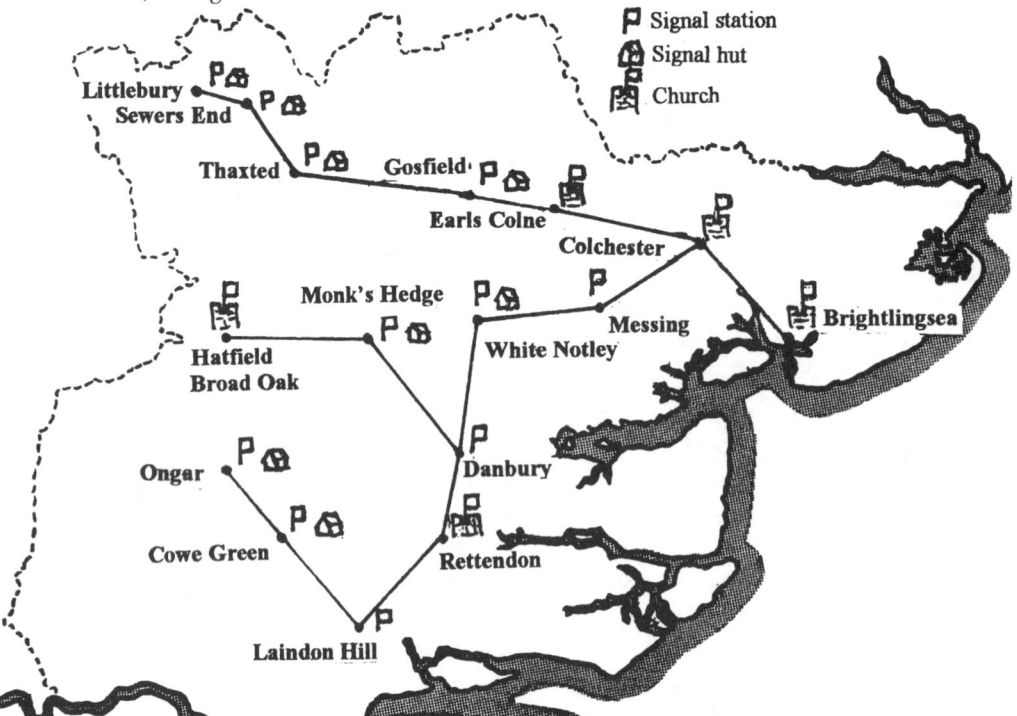

During the Napoleonic Wars a system of primary signal stations was developed to give early warning of enemy landing

On 24 July, 1801, Lord Nelson, just returned from the Baltic, was appointed commander-in-chief of the district extending from Orfordness to Beachy Head, with the Sea Fencibles and a squadron of men-of-war placed under his authority. This was the period when invasion was expected as Napoleon collected his army and flotilla at Boulogne. In Nelson's view, Essex was not likely to be the target of attack, but the more vulnerable spots were still most carefully guarded. Among the measures taken were a strong mobile squadron under Nelson to attack enemy ports. To deal with the French flotilla, if it ever reached that far, a fleet of small boats and at strategic points floating batteries both manned by the Sea Fencibles, which now totalled 1,205. Anchored behind the Gunfleet, thus closing the three passages through the sands, were two floating batteries, while placed at the mouth of the Blackwater, Colne and Orwell were river barges, each carrying four guns.

The panic of this autumn (1803) in Colchester was long remembered; to quote from a letter written at the time: -

'No thinking people at all doubt our being invaded, but as to their success there are different opinions... General Craig is still indefatigable... the Butter Market is being walled up to make a guardhouse; and everything goes on with the utmost vigour. Yesterday was the Fast; the volunteers, mayor, etc., all went to St James to hear Mr Round who preached from the Maccabees!'

There was also a widespread flight of the non-combatants. Mr Twinning, rector of St Mary's (and of Fordham) was among them, and he writes on 31 October, 1803: 'I suppose you will not ask me why I leave Colchester, I leave it because I am afraid to stay in it. Many have left, more are preparing to leave it'.

At about the same time the mediæval system of beacons was reintroduced in full force. Piles of straw, faggots, and tar-barrels were 'erected on the hill-tops at Colchester, Wigborough, Danbury, Laindon Hills, Corme Green, Ongar Park, Good Easter, Wethersfield, and Littlebury Broom'. Additionally, so that bonfires could not be mistaken for warnings, no weeds or haulm were allowed to be burnt in the fields.

Chapter 14
Tilbury, Harwich and other sites

With the introduction of the cannon and the Crown gradually taking a more responsible attitude towards national unity in the sixteenth century, castles and other protected houses were no longer needed as a practical means of defence against attack by neighbouring lords.

However, those castles still in existence during the sixteenth and seventeenth centuries and offering suitable personal living accommodation for their owners continued in use for many more years.

Defence of the realm switched from safeguarding property at home towards protection from the possibility of attack from overseas. Henry VIII saw the need for coastal defences that could withstand the primitive cannons of his day. The typical fortress of this period was a low compact building that did not dominate the surrounding countryside. It would consist of a low rectangular, or circular, tower with platforms to support the guns around it. Sometimes there would be arched casements lower down where the cannons fired through an opening.

Two forts were erected in Essex by Henry VIII, one at Tilbury, the second at Harwich. The orders for the first, at Tilbury, were issued in February, 1539, and work started almost immediately. It was finished the following year. Two blockhouses, to the design of Sir Christopher Morice and James Nedeham, were constructed at East and West Tilbury. The total cost of one blockhouse was £211 13s. 4d.(£211.67p), made up of materials - 150,000 bricks, 200 tons of chalk and an unspecified quantity of timber - £131 13s. 4d., and labour £80.

The 'D' shaped West Tilbury building, called the 'Hermitage Bulwark', guarded the Gravesend ferry crossing and was replaced later by Tilbury Fort, With a garrison of 11, its armament consisted of a demi-culverin, two sakers and a couple of smaller cannons. It never fired its guns in anger, but its claim to fame occurred during Elizabeth's reign as the site for her famous review of her troops.

During the Civil War the blockhouse at West Tilbury is said to have been used by the Parliamentarians as a check point before undergoing the structural changes later in the century, that remain to this day.

Although influenced by both Italian and French systems, the plan for the new seventeenth century fort used a defensive technique that had been around since the middle ages and was extensively used in castles. It employed bastion and at the same time, guns became more powerful so there was a return to earthworks, which offered better shock absorbing properties, as an additional form of defence. It is interesting to note that the bastion planned for the river front was never built, instead the blockhouse was retained and the curtain wall built up to it. It is possibly around this time that the blockhouse was converted into a magazine by raising it by one storey.

The Water Gate is the most impressive architectural feature of the fortifications at Tilbury
Fort. The gate house faces south and has an ashlar (square blocks of stone) façade in two
storeys. In the spandrels, or triangular spaces above the arch, are carved trophies of arms.
The gate itself is two panelled wood leaves with a wicket in the cast, or right hand, one.

The final design for the fort consisted of a polygon basic shape, together with earthworks and two moats. For extra protection, situated between the moats was a triangular shaped island, known as a ravelin - an outwork of two faces forming a salient angle outside the main ditch before the curtain.

The initial plan was to build on to the original blockhouse and construct a double moat with the inner one 150 ft wide. Unfortunately, this provided no protection from a river attack; which was discovered when the Dutch raided the Thames and Medway in 1667.

Charles II placed the work in the hands of Sir Bernard Gomme, a Dutchman, whose initial estimate for the job was £47,000. Work began in 1670 and the fort was finished 13 years later.

The first task in construction was to move the ferry house to the site where the World End pub now stands. Next, extensive piling was needed for the foundations due to the marshy ground and to raise the floors sufficiently to stop flooding. It is said that between 2,000 and 3,000 wooden piles were used. Due to the number of fortifications being built elsewhere around the coast, work was progressing slowly. So much so that the Tilbury contract in 1676 was passed to a London alderman, Sir William Pritchard. In 1680 he was awarded a second contract for finishing the brickwork, palisades, two gates and sentry boxes.

From West Tilbury the fort was approached by a series of draw-bridges, redoubt and ravelin before entering the fort through the very elaborate Water Gate, which cost over £476 to build and is faced in Portland stone. The outer triangular shaped two-storey redoubt served as the main guardhouse. The second storey floor was timbered and there were turrets located at the angles. There was an identical redoubt located at the western end of the gun lines facing the river.

Around 1694 a military engineer surveying Tilbury reported to the authorities that 'the platforms are so rotten that a gun cannot be fired but the carriage sinks into the ground and throws the shot up into the air, so that a ship may easily go by'. As a result, that same year Tilbury and a number of other forts had the oak flooring on which the guns were standing replaced by stone. Consideration was given, at the same time, for Tilbury to become the central artillery arsenal, but it lost out to Woolwich which was said to possess more advantages.

Around 1715 the total armament for the fort is said to have totalled 75 pieces. They consisted of 26 culverin and 17 demi-cannon positioned in the west gun line and one culverin and 31 demi-cannon located in the east. During 1716 a reduction in armaments in forts around the coast, was thought necessary. At Tilbury, which at the time had 161 cannon on inventory - of which 92 were considered un-serviceable - the number was reduced to 60. These large variations in numbers over a matter of months makes one wonder how discrepancies such as these could occur.

Further building occurred nearly 10 years later with the erection of a house for the master gunner, the sutier (provision merchant) and a store house. For most of this period the stronghold saw very little excitement, spending most of its days as a transit camp. Men from a number of different regiments died here - was this from the ague due to the marshy conditions? Its function changed after Culloden, in 1746, when it acted as a prison and held for a while Highlanders captured at the battle.

The fort in 1766 was reported to be in bad repair, even though it mounted 54 guns and was said to be the only fortified location in Essex.

An extension of Tilbury was considered in 1783 when one acre and three rods of land to the west of Manor Way were bought, although no use was made of the purchase. By the turn of the century there were said to be a total of 69 32-pounders protecting the fort.

Towards the end of the eighteenth century Tilbury was considered to be the only fortress necessary for the protection of the north side of the Thames, bearing in mind that the floating boom defence between Gravesend and Tilbury still existed. This was modified in 1795.

A report of the Thames defences of the time pointed out that the coastal area between Shoebury and Coalhouse Point was mainly mud with some sand making it very unattractive for beaching boats or landing troops, and it was a considerable distance from the shore to the channel itself, except at high water. The report also stated that batteries of cannon should be located at Coalhouse Point in Essex and at Hope Point and Shornemead in Kent. In addition it recommended extra guns at various points between Coalhouse and London, possible sites mentioned were Blackwall and Crawley's Wharf. Work started at the three suggested sites in 1795 and within a year the defences on the south bank were completed. The simple semi-circular fortress being erected at Coalhouse on the north side took longer, and it is reported that by 1798 the fort was provided with a five-gun battery, which together with a cross fire from guns located on the south side should give an adequate means of protection.

A defence survey by the Duke of Wellington in the middle of the next century resulted in the enlargement of the 1790 Coalhouse fort. It now became an irregular shaped fortification, capable of housing 17 32-pounder cannon, completed in 1855. In addition two smaller forts were built on either side of the river.

Later, when it was felt that Napoleon Ill might cause trouble, defences were again reviewed. The report, although saying that the forts in the main were well sited, advised rearming Tilbury fort and that the defences at Coalhouse and Shoremead should be superseded by something far stronger that was capable of resisting heavy bombardment. So the recently completed fort was knocked down and erection of a new fortress was started in 1861.

The fort consisted of a two-storied semicircular building of granite-faced casemates 14 ft (4.3 m) thick with additional earthwork protection, with the outfacing curve toward the river. It had a vaulted roof of brick and concrete, 5 ft

Coalhouse is said to be one of the finest remaining examples of an armoured casemate fort in the country. Work began on a simple semi-circular fortress in 1795, but it was not until 1798 that it was provided with a five-gun battery. A Royal Commission in 1859 recommended that the fort was remodelled and brought up-to-date, the later stages being supervised by Colonel Charles Gordon, better known for his defence of Khartoum.

(1.5 m) thick. Inside the defences were the accommodation blocks built of Kentish ragstone.

A year later the foundations were finished and in 1863 work began on the basement. On its completion in 1865 it was another three years before erection of the upper works, gun embrasures and casemates was started. It was 1888 before installation of the guns-three 9 in. guns in an open battery on the upriver side, eleven 11 in. and four 12½ in. guns in the casemates. The main weapons were rifled muzzle-loading guns with a range of 5,468 yards (5,000 m). A wide moat on the river front gave protection from any attack from that area. Immediately in front of the casemates was a dry ditch, equipped with caponiers - covered passages across the ditch of a fort - and bastions to enable defenders to give flanking fire. In the event of an assault from the land-ward side, the accommodation barracks were equipped with loopholes. Supervising the construction work during the 1860s was General Charles George Gordon, later famous as the defender of Khartoum.

Coalhouse is said to be one of the finest examples of an armoured casemate fort remaining in the country.

Due to the rapid strides being made in the development of the power and range of artillery, Coalhouse fort very soon became archaic, Being built above ground it was highly visible and as a result extremely vulnerable to attack, especially from the direction of the sea.

To overcome this deficiency, a battery, housing six breech loading guns (four 6 in. and two 10 in.) with increased range and rapid fire, was built in 1890, 1214 ft (370 m) to the north of St Catherine's Church at East Tilbury. Protection for the new battery consisted of a shallow earthwork, blended carefully into the slope, using the Twydall profile. Concealed in deep concrete-lined pits the guns were brought to the surface for firing by hydraulic units, and after firing returned below ground by the same method, thus ensuring they were exposed for the minimum time.

This method of mounting guns only had a short life span due to the cost and complexity of the system, and they were replaced by traditional artillery in 1903. Before the end of the century, 1895 in fact, smokeless powders reduced even further the opportunity for the enemy to locate the guns.

It was felt that Coalhouse still had a rôle to play. It continued in use and was brought up-to-date and modified by the introduction of a battery of four quick-firing guns in 1893. The guns were mounted 1,214 ft (370 m) to the south of the fort with the intention of preventing attacks on shipping on the river by fast assault craft. The appearance of the fort was changed in 1903 by filling in the dry ditch around the area of the casemated front and protecting the casemates by the erection an earthen bank.

Defences at Harwich are first mentioned in 1338, when a grant was made to 'the Bailiffs and good men of Harwich, who intend to enclose the town with a wall of murage for five years on things for sale...'. At the time Ipswich, envious of the town's prosperity, wanted to control Harwich Harbour with the result that the grant was revoked.

Nearly 20 years later a Royal licence was granted for the building of a town wall with a six year murage to pay for it. Later still in the century (1377 to 1399) Richard II approved a murage for walls and a castle to be built at the north east corner of the town. Permission was granted during Henry IV's reign for a levy to be raised to repair the castle, so it would appear that the fortification was built.

Defences were definitely in place in 1534 as a manuscript at the British Museum shows a number of towers facing the sea on the eastern side. Where the naval dockyard was eventually built, it is thought that the tower at the north east corner was part of the castle.

At the time that the blockhouses at Tilbury were being built on the orders of Henry VIII, the defences at Harwich were also being improved. Fortifications for Beacon Hill were being discussed, and when the Earl of Oxford carried out an inspection of the defences in 1539, he found that ditches and bulwarks had already been constructed by the townsfolk, but what was lacking was ordnance of any kind. This deficiency was fairly rapidly corrected by a supply of guns. Around the same time three forts were built. One on Beacon Hill, which was known as the 'Bulwark upon the Hill'. The second called the 'Middle House', was erected between Beacon Hill and the third fort the Ness, located at the 'Blockhouse of the Tower'. Some scholars think that the middle fort was possibly known as the 'Queen's Bulwark'.

In the year of the Armada the defences were improved and '46 great guns' positioned. It is thought that these changes resulted from the Earl of Warwick's requests a year earlier for 19 guns and £1,288 to fund repairs. These consisted of restoration of the existing walls, repairs or construction of a stone bulwark for the defence of the port, and to protect the quays the building of a palisade.

Over the years Harwich's defences fell into neglect. By 1625 it was claimed that only three or four cannon were serviceable. So disgusted was Sir Harbottle Grimston, the town's MP, that in a survey of the situation he wrote 'wee find soe greate and many decays in the former fortifications, with soe want of ordinance and all other military necessities, and the poverty of the towne to be such that it is almost impossible to impeach a resolute enymy.' Three months later improvements were carried out following an inspection by the Duke of Buckingham. These included a half moon fort of 16 rods (80.5 m) at an area called the 'Kings Keye' landing place, thought to be at the south-east corner of the town. Its dimensions were earthworks 52 ft (15.8 m) thick, a 5 ft (1.5 m) wall, and a 4 ft (1.2 m) tall parapet, which was 15 ft (4.6 m) thick at the base and 11 ft (3.3 m) thick at the top. The gate was protected by 'pallizadoes' 7 ft (2.1 m) high and 48 ft (14.6 m) long. Throughout its life the mount has been known by a number of names including Dunn Bulwark, Queen's Mount and Middle House or Bulwark. Close by was another 'pallizadoe' measuring 7 ft (2.1 m) high and 30 ft (9.1 m) long, supporting three platforms each mounting eight iron and four brass cannon. Incorporated into the latter fortification was a gunner's store and guardhouse, with, on the parapet, a sentry box and a room to house the sergeant. Its armament was said to consist of two demi cannon; 28 culverins; 17 demi culverins; 10 sakers; and one basilisk.

Landguard across the estuary from Harwich is today part of Suffolk. It was at one time considered very much a part of the Harwich port defences protecting its northern approaches.

Originally a low lying island where an invasion landing could be easily accomplished, by the time of the Armada it had silted up and fortifications were able to be erected on it. Building began in earnest in 1628 with the construction of a structure with bastions and earth ramparts, approximately 1000 yards (914.4 m) long to supersede the earlier battery. It is said that the officers on both sides, ie Landguard and Beacon Hill, were proud of their new defences. The same could not be said of officers in the Navy. Captain Richard Plumleigh complained to the Lord Admiral's secretary in 1629 of the difficulties on entering the harbour. A little later he was involved with the commandant ashore about striking his flag while at anchor and was threatened with sinking by shots fired from the shore. The commandant claiming, 'I have warrant from my Lord of Warwick to do so'. The captain, backed by his King's commission, differed and exclaimed, 'I am myself as able to beat this paper fort to pieces with my ordnance as you to sink me'. One hopes that they saw sense as no records appear to have survived describing the upshot.

As the need for shipbuilding grew so the strongholds within the town were removed or allowed to decay. The remains of the castle were demolished, and the Ness bulwark and tower blockhouse were removed to make way for the King's Building Yard, later to become the Navy yard. This resulted in Landguard becoming the harbour's major and only fortification.

The approach of the eighteenth century once again saw the fort in a derelict condition.

Following an inspection it was decided to rebuild Landguard Fort, and by 1800 the new structure housed 115 mounted guns. As happened so many times before, by the middle of the century when danger again threatened, it was found that only 12 of the weapons were serviceable. Again they were replaced, this time by five 12½ in. and five 10 in. rifled muzzle loaders and two 64-pounder converted guns, which remained in place until the early 1900s.

Towards the end of the century there were no defensive positions within the town, which looked to Beacon Hill - where major changes were taking place - and Landguard for its protection. It was proposed to install breech loading guns at both sites to protect the harbour from attacks from the sea. As Beacon Hill was vulnerable to attack from the rear it was felt additional defences were needed and an artificial hill was built as a safeguard. Also provided were a dugout for the crew and an engine room. Both these facilities were of a height to provide protection but allow the 4.7 in. guns to swivel and not obstruct their fields of fire. A slope with a ditch and fence gave cover on the landward side while the entrance was overlooked by the Redoubt. All these alterations were in place by the late 1890s.

A first for Beacon Hill was the installation of 9.2 in. and 10 in. carriage guns, which contained a mechanism, activated when the gun was in action, every two minutes raising the gun to the firing point, remaining there for 20 seconds while the gun fired, and then retracting inside its protective shell. The idea was to present to the enemy a smaller target than that offered by a casemate fort. Its major disadvantage was the expensive mechanism necessary for its operation. Also overlooked was the difficulty of an enemy hitting so small a target as a gun.

In 1798 when invasion was a real threat, the raising of a territorial defence force was announced by the Government. In Essex it was commanded by Captain Eliab Harvey, RN, from Chigwell, who was responsible for defending the coastal area from Leigh to Harwich.

Known as the 'Sea Fencibles' the men were to be recruited locally, drilled and exercised ashore, and were expected to serve a tour of duty on board ship. The most useful men to the service would be those with knowledge of the sea. As a result recruitment was difficult as men remembered the stories relating to press gangs of earlier years. After 10 years, before the wars with France were over, the force was disbanded.

During this period - between 1807 and 1810 - a large circular structure, known as the Redoubt, was constructed of hard brick set in Roman cement. Much of the work being carried out by French prisoners of war. It was about 200 ft (61 m) in diameter with walls 8 ft (2.4 m) thick and surrounded by a 20 ft (6 m) wide ditch. Most of the fortification was below ground level. Entry to the fortress was by a drawbridge, which is still the means of access today.

Its original armament consisted of 10 24-pounder guns - one of which still survives set in concrete in an embrasure on the upper level. Magazines below ground level stored the ammunition, which was supplied to the guns by five hoists. Although there was a well for the supply of drinking water within the Redoubt, a 10,000 gallon gravity fed water tank was situated outside the walls for all other applications, such as fire fighting, cleaning and so on - very vulnerable in the event of an actual landing taking place.

Additional defences - three gun batteries - were erected during 1811 to 1812, at Beacon Hill, Angel Gate and Bathside Bay. Angel Gate's field of fire covered the harbour; Bathside protected the western side of town. Originally, the Bathside D-shaped battery was by the beach overlooking the bay, but a new by-pass and land reclamation has meant that the fortress is now 150 yards (1,37.2 m) inland. Its position and layout can be seen in the verge at the side of the modern road.

Total armament for the defence of Harwich harbour at this period was the 10 guns in the Redoubt, five 24-pounders south of the Redoubt, a further five a piece at Angel Gate, and Beacon Cliff. There was another gun battery at Bathside. Today the Redoubt is scheduled as an Ancient Monument and has been restored and preserved by the Harwich Society.

Also around the early 1800s Martello towers made their appearance. While Britannia ruled the waves, the same could not be said about the land forces. Defeats on land were experienced in America, the West Indies, the Netherlands and during various raids in Europe.

A confident Napoleon was building flat bottomed boats in preparation for invading England, and actually made a couple of landings at Fishguard in Wales and Killal Bay in Ireland.

The towers came about as a result of naval experience in the Mediterranean. Corsican patriots called for assistance in driving the French from the island. The naval force sent to assist discovered that San Fiorenzo one of the anchorages selected as a suitable point for landing was protected by three old watch towers. For the raid to be successful the Mortella tower, overlooking the town, had to be taken. It was bombarded for two hours by HMS *Lowestoft* before being captured. When the navy left the Corsican patriots were unable to hold the tower and were driven out by the French. On the its return a few months later the navy found the tower was not so easy to seize the second time. Two ships took part in the action, HMS *Fortitude*, 74 guns, and HMS *Juno*, 32 guns, they suffered six killed and 60 casualties, and still the tower with 38 men, two 18-pounders and one 6-pounder resisted. It was left to the army firing continuously for two days with four guns 150 yards from the tower before the defenders eventually surrendered.

It appears that this resistance had a dramatic impact on the military minds in England. With Napoleon preparing for invasion, English thoughts now were for the protection of vulnerable coastal areas with strong forts manned by few men and guns, such as was encountered in Corsica at Mortella Point. There is some confusion as to how the name Martello came about. One school of thought says it is a result of a combination of Mortella Point which was covered with wild myrtle - spelt in Italian 'mirtillo'. Another says the name may have come from the west coast Italian watch towers - which were known as 'torri di martello' - from the striking of a bell with a hammer to sound the alarm.

Towers were built at a number of points along the south coast and between St Osyth in Essex and Aldeburgh, Suffolk. Other positions in Essex were not protected possibly due to the fact that the coast in areas such as the islands of Foulness, Mersea, the Crouch estuary and the Dengie Hundred were difficult places to effect an invasion landing. There were differences in design between the 11 individual towers built along the Essex coast possibly the result of the different builders employed.

The average Martello Tower was 33 ft high with 13 ft thick walls at its base. Entry doors, which faced inland, were situated around 14 ft above the ground with two windows normally positioned either side of the door. Today modem concrete steps give access to the Jaywick Tower door.

The windows on this tower are placed well away from the entry door, the door at ground level was added later. A photograph taken about 1913 shows a guard house and the magazine around the outside of the Jaywick Martello Tower. Today it sits forlorn surrounded by holiday caravans.

Initial work on the east coast forts started in 1808, four years later than those on the south coast. It began with the purchasing of the land and the ordering of the bricks. Each tower needed over 700,000 bricks. After all this activity and expense it is not known whether the towers would have lived up to expectations, as they were never actually used, not even later in the century when invasion threatened yet again.

The towers were lettered A to K. Those remaining are located at Seawick, (Bel Air Caravan Park) (C); Eastness, Jaywick, in the caravan park (D); Clacton Wash, (the Holiday Camp) (E). Clacton Marine Parade (F); and Walton Backwaters Caravan Park (K). The tower at St Osyth (A) was demolished in 1967 to make way for a housing development.

The towers presented a smooth surface on the outside and were round or elliptical. On average the towers were built 33 ft (10 m) high, with a diameter at the base of 58 ft (17.7 m). The thickness of the wall at this point was 13 ft (4 m) thick tapering to 6 ft (1.8 m) at the top. The entrance was located on the landward side of the building and positioned at first floor level - about 14 ft (4.2 m) from the ground. It was flanked by two windows either side. The flat leaded roof was protected by a 6 ft (1.8 m) parapet. At some sites slides were provided below the doors for materials to be brought in.

While entrance to the towers in most cases was by ladder, which could then be lifted into the building, at towers B, F, G, and J, there was a dry moat which was crossed by a drawbridge.

Inside at ground level was the basement which served as a store and magazine. It was reached by a trap door at first floor level. The first floor was divided by wooden partitioning into three, providing the living accommodation for the officer in one section, 24 privates and a sergeant in another while the third portion acted as another store room. Also from this floor a stairway led up to the second floor, the flat roof, and the gun platform. On the east coast towers it was found that a 24-pounder long gun could be mounted, together with two short 24-pounders and two 5½ in. howitzers. The long gun could be rotated. This was achieved by means of a brick pillar built inside the tower housing a pivot on which was mounted a slide supporting the oak gun carriage. Ready use ammunition was stored in six recesses located in the parapet. A typical ammunition inventory for a tower would consist of; 100 round shot for the 24-pounder gun; 20 case and grape shot for the 24-pounder gun; 40 case for the howitzers; 280 various types of shell; 40 howitzer carcasses; 80 hand grenades; 380 flannel cartridges; 120 bursters; ½ ton powder; and 1 lb slow match.

Gun batteries were installed on the seaward side at all towers except for E and H. Apart from H, each tower had a battery of three, four, or five 24-pounders in front of it. Additional protection in the form of gun batteries close to the towers was proposed, and at some stage and at some places the work was carried out. A photograph exists of tower D at Eastness, Jaywick taken in 1913 which shows the battery guardhouse and the magazine.

Traces of additional defences built in the county during the Napoleonic war can be seen at Chelmsford, in the area of Galleywood, and at Danbury. The fortification at Chelmsford, which was designed to last only a short time, was built to keep open the main supply route to London and support the coastal defences. It consisted of a linear earthwork and several detached redoubts and forts extending south from Widford through Galleywood. Another area where traces of earthworks are visible is at the west end of Danbury Common. Both sites supported thousands of troops during the war, both with camps and exercises. Once all the troops had departed the areas returned to normal and remained that way for the remainder of the century.

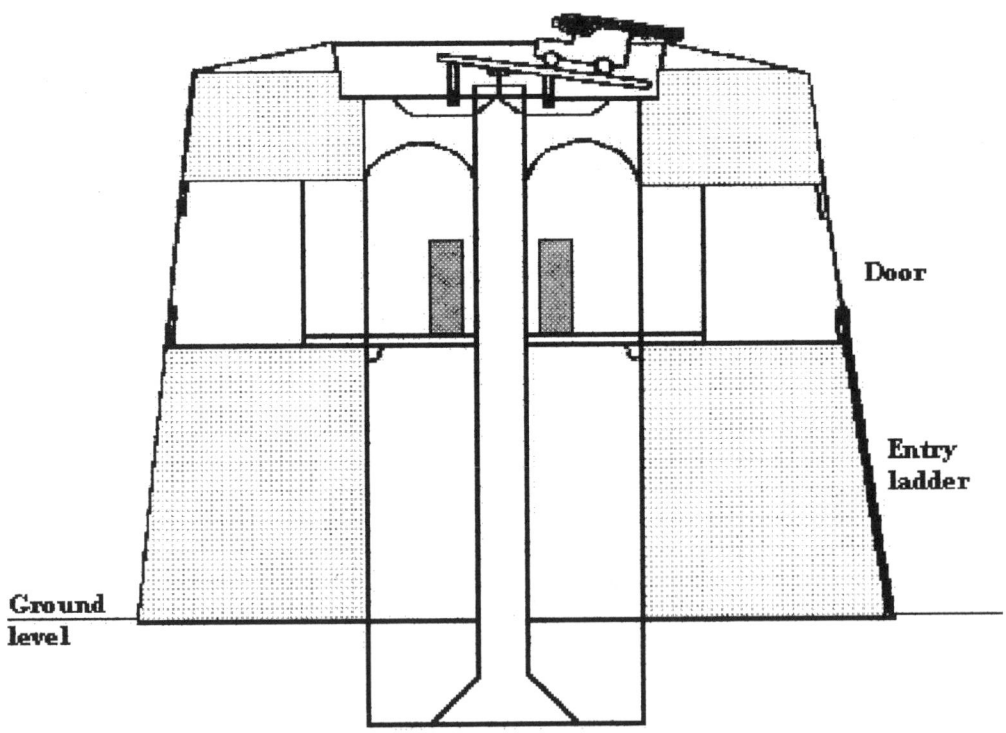

Section through a Martello Tower

Chapter 15
Essex Regiments

During the war with Spain of 1739 and before the war with France (1743) the first forerunner of the Essex Regiment came into being. The 1st Battalion, the Essex Regiment was formed in 1740 by Colonel James Long - of the 1st Foot Guards (Grenadier Guards) - as the 55th Regiment of Foot. It was one of seven extra regiments of infantry to be raised that year to augment the Regular Army. Ten years later, with the disbandment of the 43rd Regiment (American Provincial Corps) after the treaty of Aix-la-Chapelle (October, 1748), and ten Marine Regiments (44th to 53rd) no longer considered regiments of the Line, it was renumbered the 44th. It took the place of Wolfe's Regiment.

The unit was originally to be raised in the South of England, but there is no definite knowledge of the districts or the place it was assembled, although the royal warrant dated 3 January, 1741, says the men can be recruited from 'any county or part of Great Britain'. From the names of officers and extracts from other records the suggestion is that most of the men came from the Border region, Long's letter of authority stated that the regiment should consist of 'ten companies of three sergeants, two drummers and seventy effective private men in each company, besides commission officers, and to grant a warrant for allowing two pounds for each private man as levy-money'.

Two drummers and 50 privates were drafted from the 4th Foot during that February, and the following month the Secretary-at-War ordered that further men should be sent from four regiments in North Britain.

Sir Peter Halkett was lieutenant-colonel, and other officers of regiment were: William Shewen, Major; Matthew Aylmer, David Braimer, Russell Chapman, Basil Cochrane, Charles Knipe, Thomas Mason, Charles Tatton, captains (in those days the field officers were each expected to command a regiment); Durand Therond, captain-lieutenant; John Bickerstaff, John Dale, Nicholas Dunbar, Leonard Hewetson, David Kennedy, Samuel Rogers (adjutant), James Sandilands, Jesse Shaftoe, George Watson, George Welbourne, lieutenants; Michael Alcock, John Archer, William Cunningham, - Dalzell, George Davies, West Diggs, David Drummond, Sir John Elphinstone, ensigns; High Vans, quartermaster; William Trotter, surgeon; and Edmund Morris, chaplain. A letter from the War Office, dated 16 February, 1741, granting certain commissions, provides additional information concerning some of the officers.

Three were on half pay, they were Lieutenants David Braimer, Thomas Mason and Captain Shewen. Russell Chapman was a lieutenant in Colonel Ponsonby's Regiment; Basil Cochrane was the same rank in General Whetham's; Charles Tatton was an ensign in Major-General Howard's; Matthew Aylmer was an ensign in the 1st Regiment of Foot Guards; while Durand Therond was an ensign on half pay, specially designated to be captain lieutenant of the 44th. Charles Knipe was described simply as captain.

At the time of his promotion Thomas Mason must have been about 60 years old, for in 1745 he applied to the Secretary-at-War stating that he was 65 years of age, had been an officer in the Army for nearly forty years and suffered terribly from asthma and rheumatism. He continued that the previous year while on a command in the Highlands he broke two ribs and an arm, these together with his other ailments, made it difficult to carry out his duties. He was allowed to retire and the adjutant, Lieutenant Samuel Rogers succeeded him as captain.

By June the regiment had 515 men fit for service and was short of 185 to reach its establishment target. Two years later it had 751 effectives and wanted only 29 privates. By a Royal Warrant issued 1 July, 1751, the unit was authorized to wear yellow facings and to carry a regimental colour of similar hue.

Shortly after inauguration the 55th formed part of the small force in Scotland, under Lieutenant-General Sir John Cope, when Prince Charles Edward Stewart raised his standard at Glenfinnan. Its first major service was at the Battle of Prestonpans on 21 September, 1745, where the English infantry scattered following a surprise attack by the Highlanders. The regiment, under Sir Peter Halkett, offered a spirited resistance from a convenient ditch and was able to surrender on terms. Later it was to sail for America to fight the French there.

Again it suffered badly in the attack on Fort Duquesne (now Pittsburg) in 1755. General Edward Braddock led a band of British and colonial troops, including the 44th, when it was ambushed and many of the soldiers killed. The scattered remnants of the British force were saved by the clever dispositions of a young colonial officer, who became even more famous 20 years later as General George Washington.

The battalion was long known as the 'Two Fours' and the 'Little Fighting Fours', as a result of its regimental number.

While the 1st Battalion was busy in America, opposing French domination across the Atlantic, the threat still continued in Europe and the government was roused into adding 10 new regiments of infantry to the establishment, as a prelude to the Seven Years' War. Lord Charles Manners, formerly Lieutenant-Colonel to the 3rd Foot Guards, was commissioned as Colonel to raise the 58th on 26 December, 1755. Owing to two regiments being disbanded, from 1757 it became known as the 56th, with a uniform coat of scarlet, with deep crimson facings. Originally the men were recruited from the north, mainly Newcastle and Gateshead.

By 27 February, 1756, the regiment was actually in being with 10 companies, each consisting of 78 NCOs and men. An advertisement of the time read: 'All persons who are willing to serve their King and Country at this time and will engage themselves in the 58th Regiment of Foot, commanded by the Right Hon. the lord Charles Manners, now quartered at Newcastle-upon-Tyne, and recruiting in the several market towns in Northumberland, will receive for their inlisting money two guineas, free from all deductions, if they are five feet eight inches high or upwards, and one guinea and a half if they are five feet five inches high or upwards, and half a guinea more to supply them with necessaries on their joining the regiment.

'And, as a further encouragement, the Earl of Northumberland hereby offer a reward of one guinea, over and above what is given by the recruiting officer, to every able-bodied man who shall be willing to inlist in the said regiment; and shall apply for that purpose to Lieutenant-Colonel Parr, commanding officer, at Newcastle; to Mr James Scott at Alnwick Castle; to Mr Gabriel Hall at Morpeth; to Mr Robert Lowes at Hexham; or to Mr Gabriel Redhead at Rothbury, who will pay the same to each person who shall inlist accordingly. And all such persons shall have the further privilege (if it is their choice not to inlist for life) to be engaged only for the term of three years or during the continuance of a war with France; at the expiration of which they shall be entitled to their discharge.'

So many other people were willing to hand over a guinea, that in the finish a notice was published stating that in addition to the recruiting officer's disbursement the recruit would be entitled to only one further guinea.

Officers in 1756 were: Lieutenant-Colonel Peter Parr; Major John Doyne; captains, John Deaken, Thomas Hargrave, John Heighington, William Playstowe, James Stewart; William Earl of Sutherland. captain-lieutenant, Francis Gregor; lieutenants, John Archer, David Dundas, Edwin Eyre, John Forster, Thomas Harrison, John Ingram, Wilson Marshall, James Perrin, St John Pierce Lacy, John White; ensigns, Joseph Baillie, John Brereton, Christopher Hales, Edward Jenkins, Fiennes Jenkinson, James Lyons, William Sandys, Archibald Wight, John Woodford; chaplain, John Halsted; adjutant, John Hardy; quartermaster, William Lamplow; surgeon, William Pitman.

A local sensation was provided in August when it was discovered that one of the recruits was a woman from Redwater, Northumberland. 'She was set at liberty on returning the enlisting money, but seemed greatly dissatisfied that she could not be allowed to serve his Majesty in either the Army or Navy, having some time before enlisted on board a man of war.'

During the Revolutionary War in America (1775-1783), the aid that France was supplying to rebels resulted in fears of invasion again. Essex, as a result became a place of arms, the assembly point for a number of armies with camps established at Danbury, Lexden Heath, Warley, Clacton, and other areas; earthworks were thrown up, guns mounted, and volunteers enrolled. Among the troops were 10,000 Hessians - German mercenaries from the Hesse-Kassel area. It was at Warley in 1778 that George III and his Queen reviewed the regiments.

By 1764 England was once more at peace with France. At this time the regiment was stationed in Dublin and an order was issued changing the colour of the uniform facings to a shade of purple known as 'Pompadour'. This was the favourite colour of the mistress of Louis XV, Mdme Pompadour, and possibly results in the 56th being given the nickname of the 'Pompadours' or 'Saucy Pompeys'.

September, 1757, saw the ten companies reduced to nine - a grenadier and eight battalion companies - with an establishment of 42 officers, including a surgeon and two mates, and 992 non-commissioned officers and men. The latter also embraced the fifers of the grenadiers.

On 31 August, 1782, in a circular letter from the Commander-in-Chief, Field-Marshall Henry Seymour Conway, the 44th were directed to assume the title East Essex Regiment of Foot and so became linked to the county. The 56th, who were serving at Gibraltar, received the title of the West Essex. It was hoped that by giving territorial designations to the regiments it would stimulate recruiting in the counties thus honoured. The letter also pointed out that the territorial title was an alternative to the number by which the Regiment was usually known and which, coming first, continued to be used in military circles for long years thereafter: indeed, until 1881, when the short service system was introduced and the depôt was definitely located in Essex, that either the East Essex (44th) or the West Essex (56th) were mainly recruited from men of the county.

It was to replace the troops sent to serve abroad during the Seven Years' War that the formation of the county militia in 1759 was brought about. At first the quota fixed for each of the Essex battalions was 480, and arms for them were delivered from the Tower of London on 23 June, 1759. In November the two battalions that had been formed were quartered at Ely, St Ives, Caxton and Huntingdon.

In 1778 the eastern regiment of Essex Militia, commanded by Colonel Isaac Rebow, was at Coxheath. Four years later the regiment consisted of nine companies, eight raised by ballot, and one by volunteers, and numbered 615 of all ranks, commanded by John Bullock. The West Essex in 1778 occupied Chatham barracks under the earl of Rochford. In 1782 the regiment mustered 618 of all ranks in nine companies all raised by ballot. Their commander was Sir William Smith (or Smyth). In July that year East Essex were at Harwich and the West Essex at Lenham Hall.

On renewal of hostilities after the Peace of Amiens, the East Essex regiment was stationed in Ireland and while it was garrisoned there a second battalion was raised, which proved worthy of affiliation to the county. It served with distinction throughout the Peninsular campaign, in particular when it captured the eagle of the 62nd French infantry - which can now be seen at Chelmsford museum. Later on further honours were heaped on it with an heroic stand at Quatre Bras two days before the Battle of Waterloo, when it withstood a charge of the French lancers in line, instead of a square, beat them off, and helped save the situation.

Colchester Barracks, 1856

The Essex Regiment on parade in 1894

Eventually Napoleon's overthrow at Waterloo on 18 June, 1815, had assured the peace throughout Europe with the result that naval and military establishments were speedily reduced. Among those to disappear quickly was the second battalion 44th Foot the East Essex regiment.

On the home front throughout the remainder of the century nothing happened of note militarily. Overseas the two Essex regiments played their part. In 1841-2, the East Essex regiment after forming part of the Kabul garrison, was practically annihilated during the winter retreat. Later on it fought at Sebastopol in the Crimea (1855), and took part in the capture of Taku Forts in the Second China (Opium) War (1857) in which two Victoria Crosses were won. In South Africa, at the fighting round Cronje's laager (1900), Lieutenant F N Parsons won the VC, and they took part in a spirited bayonet charge at Driefontein.

Until the siege of Sebastopol life for the West Essex or 56th Foot, was relatively uneventful. It went on, after its purple facings were replaced by white, to participate in the Nile Campaign of 1884-5, the Boer War, and as the Essex Regiment in Sudan and the South African wars.

Other changes were taking place to the munitions industry in the county. Until 1872 only black gunpowder had been made at Waltham Abbey, now guncotton - discovered by the German Schönbein in 1846 - started to be made by a method developed at the factory by Sir Fredrick Abel. The old saltpetre refinery buildings housed the new guncotton factory, and it was capable of producing 250 tons/year. In 1885 'brown' or 'cocoa' gunpowder production began following its introduction from Germany, to be followed in 1891 by a smokeless powder, called Cordite, consisting of a mixture of nitroglycerine, guncotton and a mineral jelly. Before the end of the century a second plant had to be built on the site to handle the production of nitroglycerine to meet the demands for cordite.

Over nearly 10,000 years tremendous changes occurred in the way people defended themselves against attacks. At first it was protection against stone throwing. As each new weapon was developed so a suitable form of defence had to be found. In the early years the main dangers originated with settlers arriving from other areas bringing new ideas with them for both living and fighting. Gradually these techniques were absorbed, and as the time passed and it came nearer to the present day, so the tempo increased and so did the way people lived and fought. Through it all the people were determined to protect those things they loved and cherished. As can be seen Essex people were no exception, although at times there was a reluctance to take part.

During the 20th century, changes to the way people lived, and the weapons and wars in which they were involved, changed so rapidly, that it will take another book similar to this to tell the story of Essex in times of strife in the 1900s. The building of airfields, the radar stations, and how village churches played their part, are all involved in this Essex story that continues to this day.

INDEX